CW01083949

SS CANBERRA
1957 - 1997

Best Wishes

Neil McCart

Neil McCart

To the memory of a great ship

Front Cover: A magnificent watercolour painting of the *Canberra* by Mr Brian Conroy, Greatham, Hampshire.

Back Cover: The end of the story. Watched by local students the *Canberra* lies beached and waiting to be broken up at Gaddani, near Karachi, Pakistan. The photograph was taken shortly after her arrival. *(Reuters/Popperfoto)*

Cover Design by Louise McCart
© Neil McCart/FAN PUBLICATIONS 1998
ISBN: 1 901225 00 3

Typesetting By: Highlight Type Bureau Ltd,
Clifton House, 2 Clifton Villas,
Bradford, West Yorkshire BD8 7BY

Printing By: The Amadeus Press Ltd,
517 Leeds Road, Huddersfield,
West Yorkshire HD2 1YJ

Published By FAN PUBLICATIONS
17 Wymans Lane, Cheltenham, GL51 9QA, England. Fax & Tel 01242 580290

A beautiful aerial view of the *Canberra* at sea. Her classic lines set the trend for today's modern cruise ships.

(FotoFlite)

Contents

Introduction

For 37 years the *Canberra* has been a very familiar sight in Southampton's Western Docks and in ports the world over, particularly Sydney which, it could be said, has been her second home. In April 1982 the unthinkable happened when Britain went to war in hopefully the last colonial campaign in her history and for the first time in 42 years a P&O liner was requisitioned for service as a troop transport. During the three months of the Falklands campaign she made headlines the world over, and she became a household name as she continued her peacetime role. However, her career had not always been so secure and for a few months in 1972 it seemed she was destined prematurely for the scrapyard. Had that come about she would probably be remembered today as P&O's 'great white elephant', the liner which it had been thought would shape the future but, instead, had fallen victim to the age of the jet airliner and steeply rising oil prices. Fortunately she was reprieved and over the next 25 years she weathered the difficult transition from mail liner to cruise ship. She became the country's favourite, with a faithful clientele who would not sail in any other vessel. More importantly, as Australia sheds her ties with Britain, the *Canberra* represents the last in a long line of P&O passenger ships which were built to serve that continent. Not only does her passing represent the end of an important chapter for the P&O company, but it brings down the final curtain on 145 years of British maritime history.

Neil McCart
Cheltenham
April 1998

Chapter One

Before The *Canberra*

On 25 June 1996, only three years away from the end of the twentieth century, the P&O company announced that 'Britain's favourite cruise ship', SS *Canberra*, would be withdrawn from service on 30 September 1997. The announcement came as no great surprise to most of the maritime world for the ship was 35 years old, which is a good age by any standards. What was not emphasized was the fact that not only was this the end of an era for the P&O company, but it also signalled the passing of a British maritime tradition with the *Canberra* being the last in a long line of fast passenger liners which owed their origins to two small steamships, the *Chusan* and the *Formosa*, which inaugurated P&O's passenger and cargo service to Australia in 1852. It is not easy today to appreciate that in that very year the last prison ships were transporting convicts to Van Diemans Land (Tasmania) and while prisoners would continue to be sent to Western Australia for another 16 years, this sordid episode in the country's history was drawing to a close and 'free settlers' were arriving in New South Wales in increasing numbers. The main attraction for many in the mid-1800s was the discovery of gold in the newly formed state of Victoria and thousands of prospectors descended on the diggings at Ballarat and Bendigo. During the gold rush era the population of Australia doubled in the space of just a few years, and this increase inevitably generated the problem of 'disillusioned returnees', many of whom went back to Britain much worse off than they had been when they left home. But this two-way trade and the awarding of the government mail contract to Adelaide, Melbourne and Sydney in 1853 ensured the success of P&O's new passenger service.

During the latter half of the nineteenth century P&O's Australian mail service grew in importance and by 1900 the company's biggest, fastest and most prestigious ships were employed on the route. In the nine years between 1903 and 1912 ten new steamships of the 'M' class, all of them between 9,500 and 12,400 gross tons, entered service, but then in 1914 the whole service came to a standstill as the company's ships were requisitioned by the Government for service as troop transports or armed merchant cruisers. By the end of the Great War the P&O company had, like the country as a whole (and, for that matter, like most European countries), suffered grievous losses in both manpower and equipment and the task of rebuilding the fleet began. However, despite the fact that the P&O fleet was sadly depleted, the company's trade routes remained intact and with the backlog of trade to be dealt with and a temporary rise in emigration to Australia, it was not long before the company had regained the ground lost during the years in which the great European powers were tearing themselves apart.

During the inter-war years the Australian service once again dominated the company's trade and in the late 1920s a new ship-building programme was embarked upon to construct five vessels which would not only provide replacements for the Edwardian 'M' class ships which had survived the war, but which would also set new standards for the company and for the service to Australia.

The *Strathnaver* was the last of P&O's liners to be released by the Government following the end of the Second World War. She is seen here at Sydney during the 1950s. *(P&O)*

The first of the new liners, the 22,270 gross ton *Strathnaver*, entered service in October 1931 and for the first time in the company's history the emphasis was on second class passengers, now renamed tourist class. This change of emphasis reflected the fact that, although many emigrants wanted a relatively cheap passage to Australia, they were also demanding higher standards of accommodation. The last of P&O's 'Five White Sisters', the *Strathallan*, entered service in March 1938, two days before German troops crossed the border into Austria. Once again the clouds of war were gathering over Europe.

It is perhaps worth recalling memories of one of the *Strathallan's* last peacetime voyages between Tilbury and Sydney, plying a route which had been used by P&O liners for many years and enjoying a way of life which would soon be swept away for ever. George Shaw, who eventually retired from the company as a personnel manager, joined the *Strathallan* as a bellboy for her voyage which started from Tilbury on 16 September 1938. George signed on for a monthly wage of £3.4s.6d (£3.22$^1/_2$), from which he had to buy his uniforms, and reported on board to the Second Steward. The stewards' accommodation in the peak was full so he was berthed in converted passenger cabins in the tourist class section of H Deck, together with about a dozen others. He recalls that, 'We boasted a porthole, but its low level above the waterline meant it had to be closed when any sort of sea was running. Very little time was allowed for the formalities of settling in and as it was embarkation day there was not much chance of seeing your bunk until very much later on. Embarkation took place in the afternoon with all hands turned to guiding passengers to their cabins and carrying their hand luggage for them. It was my first experience of being tipped, mostly sixpences (2$^1/_2$p). Then there were the telegrams, so much a feature of sailing day at that time, to be delivered to cabins, an exercise on which I spent much energy that first time, because decks and cabins were still a mystery. It was 'Munich time' and the farewells of those who had come to see their loved ones off were that much more poignant. It was not long before the first meal of the voyage was served and as the tourist class dining saloon filled up, it became alive to a level of babble and chatter which would last for the next month, when the last passengers disembarked at Brisbane.

My day started at 6.30am, when the nightwatchman woke everybody and, after grabbing a cup of coffee, we 'ticked on' with the Leading Steward. First trippers were usually allocated jobs aft in the tourist class where there were rosters for watching the bell-board in the pantry, operating the lifts, delivering the 'wireless news', which had been typed on Gestetner skins and duplicated in the bureau, and fetching and carrying for dining saloon waiters. There were also stand-by duties at the bureau to deliver the Purser's messages to officers or passengers. The excitement of all this soon gave way to the effect of seasickness as the ship rounded Ushant and entered 'the Bay'. The awfulness of this had been smugly forecast by those who no longer suffered and an old Goan pantryman, who had seen my distress, guaranteed his 'cure' - a pint of sea water and dry biscuits. I must have been the exception because I endured a state of misery until the ship cleared Cape St Vincent. We were in and out of Gibraltar one morning, with snatched views of the grandeur of the Rock and after lunch we steamed into Tangier with the unforgettable sight of the small white buildings climbing up the hills from the shoreline. We did not go alongside and the few passengers who embarked and disembarked were handled by tender.

Our next port of call was Marseilles, where we went alongside and spent the night. Passengers taking advantage of the day and a half journey from London, instead of our four or five days' passage, came on board, along with the mail. Malta was our next port of call where we were moored to a buoy in Grand Harbour alongside an Italian liner with a considerable number of troops on board, bound for Ethiopia.

Next came one of the 'events' of the voyage, the Suez Canal transit. We went to buoys not far from the Canal Authority's offices and we were soon besieged with bumboats and a proliferation of 'Jock Mackenzies' who did their best to prise a few shillings from the novices. There was much activity however, with the embarkation of the Canal Pilot, who was held in some awe, sundry assistants and a large team of Egyptian 'fellahs' whose boat was brought inboard onto the fore well deck. For most of the time they seemed to be in a state of repose in odd corners around the forecastle. Some passengers left the ship to do sightseeing tours to Cairo and the Pyramids, and rejoined at Port Suez after our transit. During the slow passage south I strived to see as much as possible of the ship's wave rushing along the canal bank, and the scenic spots such as Ismailia and the Bitter Lakes. Within a day or two of our departure from Port Said we called at Port Sudan, a hot, dusty place and I have recollections of the local workers carrying our cargo, including enormous crates, on their backs, a mass of hair standing out as they staggered down the quay on spindly legs under a blazing sun. It was at this time that my left hand became infected and swollen and the Assistant Surgeon, in those days before antibiotics, decided to make an incision to deal with the problem. This coincided with the stifling heat of the Red Sea and I had to take a few days off duty. It gave me an opportunity to see a breathtaking view of Jeddah with its Arabic houses, which could be seen clearly as the ship went close in. We also saw a number of isolated islands, baking in the intense heat, their only occupants being lighthouse keepers.

Our next call was Aden with its searing heat, looking stark, burnt-out and barren. There were another lot of bumboats and this time I bought two Japanese-made silk

In 1949 the brand new liner *Himalaya* joined the P&O fleet and she remained a very popular ship with both passengers and crew right through to 1974 when she was withdrawn from service. *(FotoFlite)*

shirts for 1/6d (7¹/₂p) each. "Wait until we clear the Gulf of Aden and the weather will be cooler", said the pundits, and thankfully they were right, but our arrival in Bombay coincided with the onset of the monsoon weather with torrential rain and uncomfortable humidity. We berthed at Ballard Pier, the ship being assisted by some noisy tugs, and this was the port where a large number of the first class passengers disembarked to take up the reins of the "white man's burden" after home leave. Passenger trains with such glamorous names as the "Frontier Mail" were waiting for those going up-country, with a mass of porters to transfer the baggage. Milling crowds were everywhere and there was much excitement amongst our Indian crew, who were now in their home port. They were from a variety of religions, Catholic Goan stewards and Hindu Lascars on deck in their neat blue uniforms and distinctive headwear. I was becoming increasingly aware of their titles such as Serangs, Tindals, Caddabs and Bhandaries. However, despite the bedlam of Bombay there was an air of timelessness about it. After a couple of days steaming we arrived at Colombo, where a much more relaxed atmosphere prevailed and during the afternoon I walked out of town to some botanical gardens where exotic plants and wildlife abounded.

Our departure from Colombo signalled the longest sea passage of the voyage, nine days to Fremantle, which was broken only by a diversion to the Cocos Islands, where there was a wireless station and it was customary for P&O ships to drop a barrel of mail and supplies overboard. Two or three boats were there to meet us and we all gazed down on them, while the occupants seemed to be willing us to stay. All we could give them were a couple of engine movements to provide them with a lee and drop their

barrel, which drifted astern as the *Strathallan* slowly manoeuvred ahead.

During this long sea passage there was a relaxed air on board, and one of the bellboys' jobs was to attend to clearing up the first class lounge, where dancing went on until after 11pm. One of the favourites was the "Lambeth Walk" and I recall the Purser, Mr Aries, performing the dance particularly well. There was little in the way of organized entertainment, although the tourist class had an occasional film on deck and it was possible to sneak a view from behind the canvas screens which were rigged up.

There was an air of expectancy as we made landfall off Australia and docked at Fremantle on 18 October 1938, and after leaving that port we were at sea for three days before arriving at Adelaide. From there we went to Melbourne, but Sydney was our main port of call where, on 27 October, we went alongside Circular Quay, in the shadow of the Harbour Bridge which, at that time, had not long been opened. It was an irresistible attraction to walk across and I lost no time in doing so, and for a few pence I got a ferry to Manly Beach.'

After steaming on to Brisbane the *Strathallan* retraced her route back to Tilbury and the mood of the time is recalled by George Shaw: 'I remember there was much concern at the imminence of war, and in addition to the usual boat drill we had exercises in "blacking out" the ship. We finally berthed at Tilbury on 23 December 1938 and I paid off with over £11 in wages. Two large white fivers, their numbers duly recorded, were handed to me and I felt rich that Christmas.'

Just over eight months after the *Strathallan* completed her second round voyage between London and Australia the Second World War broke out and, once again, the passenger liners of the P&O were requisitioned by the Government for service as troopships and auxiliary cruisers. The Australian Commonwealth declared war with Germany at virtually the same time as the British Government, and once again Australia played an important part both in Greece and in North Africa while the liners of the P&O were engaged in the essential trooping operations from Australian ports. On 10 January 1940, the *Strathnaver*, now painted in a dull battleship grey, left Sydney with four Orient Line ships all packed with troops and bound for the Middle East.

During the first 21 months of the war, with the fighting confined to Europe and the Middle East, there was a certain amount of nervousness in Australia about the fact that almost the whole of their army was stationed a long way away from home, but they were assured by the politicians in Britain that, in the case of war in the Far East, the mother country would come to their aid. Apart from a few, very senior, politicians most people accepted these assurances and it was believed that, in the event of war with Japan, a British fleet based in the 'impregnable fortress' of Singapore would ensure the safety of Australia and New Zealand. However, in early December 1941, with the Japanese attack on the US fleet at Pearl Harbor and the subsequent invasion of Malaya and the Philippines, very suddenly the war was brought much closer to Australia's shores. The ferocity of the Japanese army and the speed and ease with which it advanced took the Allies by surprise, and

after the fall of the Singapore garrison it became painfully obvious that Australia could no longer rely on the Royal Navy, or on Britain, for its defence against external aggression. At the peak of the Japanese offensive their aircraft bombed Darwin and Broome, and almost reached Port Moresby at the south-eastern tip of New Guinea. In the event the major role in the Pacific war was borne by the United States, although the Australian Army fought its way back to the north coast of New Guinea, but Australia's weakness, particularly in manpower, was plain for the world to see. It was against this general background that Australia's post-war immigration policy was conceived.

When the Second World War finally ended in September 1945 Britain was virtually bankrupt and most of Europe lay in ruins as, for the second time in just over 30 years, the continent had torn itself apart in a major war. The British Government was faced with conflicting needs; it was vital that the country's trade returned to its pre-war levels as quickly as possible and to achieve that there was an urgent requirement for merchant shipping. However, with British troops stationed in bases and garrisons all over the world, and with the vast majority of these being 'hostilities only' conscripts, there was also an urgent need to get the armies home again as quickly as possible, not only for reasons of welfare, but also to help overcome the shortages of labour within the country's manufacturing industry. It was this latter duty which was to keep liners of the P&O fleet on government service for up to four years after the end of the war. It was, in fact, in January 1950 that the last

1954 saw the entry into service of the two handsome liners *Arcadia* and *Iberia*. The *Arcadia* remained in the company's service until 1979 when she was withdrawn and replaced by the converted Swedish liner *Sea Princess* (*Victoria*). (*FotoFlite*)

of P&O's big liners, the *Strathnaver*, made her first post-war voyage on the company's account, and by that time the post-war trade patterns had changed significantly from those of 1939 and there would be no going back.

During the war P&O had lost six of its passenger liners and, although orders had been placed for two new large vessels, with the cost of shipbuilding having risen so steeply, it was clear that the post-war rebuilding programme would not be on the scale of that undertaken during the 1920s and 1930s. There were two main factors which affected P&O's trade east of Suez and one of these was the granting of independence to Britain's Indian Empire, which meant the substantial loss of trade as the large numbers of military and government passengers suddenly ceased. In the Far East generally the British debacle at Singapore in February 1942 had had a far-reaching effect on the inhabitants of all European colonies in the region, and there was a rising tide of nationalism throughout South-East Asia. The second factor, which was much more positive, was the growing list of people wishing to emigrate from Britain and its immediate post-war austerity, all the shortages, rationing and monotonous queues, to a new life in Australia. In those days would-be emigrants could only travel such long distances by sea and it was clear that the demand for berths had outstripped the accommodation which was available. As an added bonus for the shipowners, the Australian Government, having realized how close the country had been to invasion in 1942, was keen to encourage new settlers in order to increase its population and thereby boost its economy. So keen was the Australian Government that it offered immigrants the Assisted Passage Scheme or, as it became popularly known in Australia, the 'Ten Pound Pom' scheme.

For an outlay of just £10 per person would-be emigrants could travel to the other side of the world in order to start their new lives, with the balance of the passage money being paid by the Australian Government. With Australian migration officers located at many points in the cities and towns throughout the British Isles, the initial contact was made both easy and inexpensive for the prospective migrants, the vast majority of whom had never travelled very far from home before. At the same time there were other migrants from Europe, Greeks, Italians, Ukranians, Lithuanians, Latvians and others of eastern European origin, many of whom had been uprooted and displaced during the course of the war in Europe. To cater for as many of these people as possible, P&O added Naples and Piraeus to its itinerary.

It was the sheer number of migrants from Europe to the antipodes which gave a new lease of life to four of P&O's older pre-war liners, *Mooltan*, *Maloja*, *Chitral* and *Ranchi*, all of which were converted to 'one-class tourist' and were almost exclusively booked, between 1948 and 1953, by the Australian Government. In 1954, with the arrival of the *Arcadia* and *Iberia*, all four of the older pre-war ships were sold for scrap and the *Strathnaver* and *Strathaird* were converted to tourist class vessels. In the mid-1950s, despite a worrying trend on the North Atlantic where the numbers of people travelling by air was rapidly overhauling those crossing by sea, very few could foresee a time when the ocean liners would not reign supreme on the passenger routes of the world. In addition there were still thousands of Assisted Passage Migrants waiting to emigrate to Australia. The future for P&O's traditional trade route between London and Australia appeared to be secure for the foreseeable future.

However, far from being complacent, the P&O board were looking to expand the company's trading operations and a major factor in the minds of the directors was the lucrative cruise trade in the Pacific Ocean, particularly along the West Coast of North America. The Orient Line, which was part of the P&O Group, was extending its voyages to Australia into the Pacific, and it was decided to combine the P&O and Orient Line fleets to provide three new routes which would cover the Pacific Ocean. The first would extend the traditional Australian voyages beyond Sydney to create a new service linking Australia, New Zealand and the West Coast of North America. The second would extend P&O's Far East voyages to link Hong Kong and Japan with North America, while the third route would be a triangular service between Australia, Asia and the United States.

These new routes meant much longer voyages and so greater speeds were needed in order to shorten the sailing times. If pre-war *Strath* liners were replaced by similar vessels to the *Arcadia* and *Iberia*, it was doubtful whether the required speeds would be attained and, with the increased building costs, it would have been impossible to make them pay. It was clear that the technical requirements for the new Pacific services demanded much larger and faster ships, but at the same time vessels which could negotiate both the Suez and Panama Canals and be handled at the major ports between London and Sydney.

In early 1956 P&O sent out the specifications which were required to a number of UK shipbuilders, including John Brown & Co Ltd of Clydebank, and Harland & Wolff Ltd of Belfast. The new vessel was to have a gross tonnage of 45,000 and a speed of $27^{1}/_{2}$ knots, with accommodation for about 600 first class and 1,650 tourist class passengers, which is an indication of the reliance placed by the company on the Assisted Passage Migrants. The vessel was to have an overall length of 814ft, a beam of 102ft, and her range without refuelling would be 10,000 miles. It would be over four years before these bare figures were translated into the magnificent new passenger liner, *Canberra*.

Chapter Two

Born In Belfast

When Denis Rebbeck, the deputy managing director of Harland & Wolff, received Inquiry No 29/56 from P&O he knew that what was required was a remarkable passenger liner, as the outline specifications indicated that there would be many significant changes from tradition which represented a very bold step in ship design. It was also obvious that it was to be a very prestigious order, for the new ship would be the largest merchant vessel to come out of a British shipyard since the *Queen Elizabeth* was built on Clydeside in the late 1930s. There was, then, an immense satisfaction and enthusiasm throughout Belfast when, on Thursday 20 December 1956, P&O indicated to Harland & Wolff that they would be awarded the contract for the new liner. One

month later, on Wednesday 23 January 1957, the order for job number 1621 was officially placed and preparations were made to clear a slipway so that work could begin.

The Belfast shipyard was certainly no stranger to the construction of passenger-carrying vessels, and their lists were full of famous names such as the White Star Line's *Olympic* and *Britannic*, and, of course, the ill-fated *Titanic*. For the Union Castle Line they had built the *Cape Town Castle* and the *Pendennis Castle*, and for the Shaw Savill Line there was the *Southern Cross*, which broke new ground by having her main propulsion machinery, and her funnel, placed right aft. In the late 1920s they had received an order from the White Star Line for a 1,000 ft liner which was to be named *Oceanic*, but the Depression caused the cancellation

Still surrounded by scaffolding the *Canberra* dominates the Harland & Wolff shipyard as she lies on the slipway.

(Ulster Folk & Transport Museum)

of a vessel which would have almost equalled the size of Cunard's *Queen Mary* and *Queen Elizabeth*. These are just a few of the hundreds of ships which had been built by Harland & Wolff, whose association with P&O had started in the late 1870s when they had been awarded the contract for the building of the 3,500-ton, steam-propelled schooner *Rosetta*. She had been completed in August 1880 for the Australian mail service, with accommodation for 130 first and 54 second class passengers, and she went on to serve the company for 20 years.

The first keel plates for yard number 1621 were laid on Monday 23 September 1957, at slipway No 14 in the company's Musgrave Shipyard at Queen's Island, which was where the Royal Navy's biggest post-war warship, the aircraft carrier HMS *Eagle*, was built in the years just after the Second World War. One of the first tasks to be undertaken was the dredging of the launching and fitting-out berths for the new liner and, once the building had started, the organization of supplies of steel and aluminium, and the phasing of orders for the thousands of fixtures and fittings which would be supplied by subcontractors.

It was not so much the size of the new ship which caused such excitement in the shipping world, but the fact that her main propulsion machinery was to be placed aft and, instead of one or two large and powerful looking funnels being sited amidships, two slim, streamlined uptakes were to be placed side by side at the after end of the superstructure. In fact, prior to the final choice being made, experiments had been carried out using a number of 'wing-like' funnels which were probably considered a little too futuristic looking for the 1950s as the ideas were never followed up.

Another outstanding feature of the building of the new vessel was the extent to which aluminium was used in the superstructure. The use of about 1,000 tons of this metal enabled a saving to be made in the structural weight of about 1,500 tons, which meant that accommodation for over 200 additional passengers could be installed. More than 800 tons of aluminium plates and extrusions were provided by the British Aluminium Co Ltd, and a further 200 tons of aluminium plate, which included all the material for the Games Deck, was supplied by Alcan Industries. The use of such large quantities of the metal created problems with welding, which had to be carried out at high speeds using special equipment. In all, four tiers of the passenger accommodation, together with a further four tiers of the bridge superstructure, were constructed from

Dame Pattie Menzies pulls the launching lever and a bottle of Australian wine is sent crashing down onto the *Canberra's* bulbous bow. Seconds later the liner would be thundering down the slipway and into the waters of the Walney Channel. *(P&O)*

aluminium, as were the mast and the twin funnels.

As the construction work progressed at Harland & Wolff's Belfast yard, P&O's publicity programme ensured that the liner was regularly featured in the news media, and on Monday 17 March 1958 one of the shipping industry's best kept secrets - the name which was to be given to the revolutionary new liner - was revealed by Sir Donald Anderson, deputy chairman of P&O. Appropriately Sir Donald was in Australia at the time and, even more appropriately, he was attending a dinner with the country's leading political correspondents in Australia's administrative capital, Canberra. First of all he reminded his audience that the new liner was the biggest to be built in Britain since the Cunard 'Queens' and that the ship was arousing almost as much interest during the construction stages as did the *Queen Mary* some 24 years previously. He teased his fellow guests by reminding them that the name of Cunard's mighty ship was known to no one but her owners until the moment she was launched, and that many thought that P&O's great new liner would remain 'Yard No 1621', until launching day. Fortunately he broke the suspense and received rapturous applause from his audience when he announced that the new liner would be named *Canberra*, after Australia's capital. The choice of name was an inspired public relations exercise as the P&O company, in common with other British fleets in the Australian trade, had received a certain amount of hostile criticism since the

The whole of Harland & Wolff's shipyard comes to a standstill as all the workers watch the *Canberra's* great hull take to the water.

(P&O)

end of the war in 1945, and the naming of the flagship after Australia's capital city symbolized the common bonds between Australia and Britain. Sir Donald went on to explain that since the end of 1945 P&O had invested almost half a million pounds in Australia, and that the name had been chosen to symbolize the part P&O had played in Australia's development. The name itself is an Aboriginal word which means 'meeting place' and over the next 37 years the ship herself would certainly live up to it. Sir Donald announced that the *Canberra*, together with the new Orient liner, *Oriana*, would form the nucleus of a British passenger fleet which would enter the north, central and southern Pacific trade under the name of Orient & Pacific Lines, operated jointly by P&O and the Orient Line. Finally he ended his speech by stating: 'In building this new ship the P&O company is assuming the continuance of British migration to Australia, and the need for passenger ships to carry them in the most up-to-date conditions. A continuation of an active migration programme is necessary for the company to justify the investment of £15 million sterling in this ship. We estimate that a ship of this size and cost cannot be made to operate at a profit on the United Kingdom-Australia trade alone, but we look to adequate earnings by extending voyages across the Pacific. We believe that Australia is the keystone of the Pacific in development over the next 50 years.' Once again P&O's post-war reliance on migration to support its passenger trade was emphasized.

During 1958 the *Canberra* enjoyed all manner of publicity, and at the 31st World Fair in Brussels, where the British pavilion was the fifth largest site in the exhibition, covering some 500 acres, an 8ft-6in scale model of the liner was put on display. It was the first time that the model had been seen in public and it was intended to demonstrate the extent to which electricity was used at sea. The P&O exhibit attracted a great deal of interest and visitors were delighted by its many 'working' devices. Perhaps the most popular of these was the telephone system which gave descriptions of the *Canberra* in three languages, English, French and German. A display panel floodlit the model both internally and externally and separate models showed how cargo would be loaded and unloaded, and how the lifeboat davit mechanism worked.

In August 1958 telegrams were exchanged between the P&O company and the US Navy, on the occasion of an anniversary which linked Britain, Australia and the USA. In August 1942, the cruiser HMAS *Canberra* was lost during the night action with the Japanese Navy off Savo Island in the South Pacific. In the following year, as a tribute to the Australian warship, the US Navy named a newly built heavy cruiser, USS *Canberra*. The telegram from the commanding officer of the USS *Canberra*, which had been modernized as a guided missile cruiser and recommissioned in June 1956, read as follows: 'Sixteen years ago the gallant Australian cruiser *Canberra* was sunk off Savo Island. This anniversary is an appropriate occasion to send greetings to you the builders of another *Canberra* whose name symbolizes the ocean links between Britain and Australia as does ours, these same bonds between Australia and the United States. We hope for a proud moment in the future when our ships will exchange greetings on the high seas.' The reply from P&O head office in London's Leadenhall Street read: 'We reciprocate your friendly greetings and look forward to the day when USS *Canberra* and SS *Canberra* "dip ensigns" to one another and together pay homage to their gallant precursor, HMAS *Canberra*. Three ships, three nations linked together by one name in hope and enterprise on the high seas.' Already, more than two and a half years before she entered service, the *Canberra* was bringing the nations and the continents together.

That same month the *Canberra* became the centre of attraction at Olympia Stadium in London, when the Brussels model was put on display at the Schoolboys' and Schoolgirls' Exhibition. Situated as it was, right next door to the Royal Navy's stand, the 'Senior Service' had their thunder stolen by P&O's new liner. Meanwhile in Australia, at the Queensland Centenary Celebrations, another scale model of the *Canberra* was on show and one of the thousands of admirers was Princess Alexandra, who was the sponsor of the *Oriana*. However, the main news that summer was that Dame Pattie Menzies GBE, wife of Sir Robert Menzies the Australian Prime Minister, had consented to launch the *Canberra* and, in addition, she was to make a special visit to Britain in order to do so. However, with industrial problems at Harland & Wolff's shipyard, *Canberra's* building schedule was starting to fall behind and the launch, which had originally been intended for November 1959, was postponed until 1 March 1960. Unfortunately this date too had to be cancelled, with the ceremony finally being set for Wednesday 16 March 1960.

Dame Pattie Menzies left Sydney on 23 January 1960 in the *Arcadia* and apart from a delay in the Mediterranean with engine trouble, the voyage to London passed off without any serious problems and the *Arcadia* arrived in Tilbury on Thursday 25 February, three weeks before the launching ceremony.

The day itself, which was the eve of St Patrick's Day, dawned as a somewhat grey and drizzly morning at Belfast, with the only brightness being the *Canberra's* great white hull which towered over slipway 14. The enormous hull, bedecked with flags, was fully visible for the first time now that the scaffolding which had enveloped her for so long had been removed. However, it was four years on from those days in early 1956 when the idea of the *Canberra* had been first discussed and there was a distinct feeling in the air that the launch of a big passenger ship would soon be just a distant memory. The jet airliner had arrived in the

As soon as she had been steadied in the water the tugs were able to take *Canberra* in tow and move her slowly round to her fitting-out berth alongside the Thompson Wharf.
(Belfast Telegraph)

form of BOAC's Comet 4 and Boeing's enormously successful 707 aircraft. Both aircraft were suddenly reducing the flying time between London and Sydney and also, for the first time, reducing the cost of air fares. Although the short-term future for passenger liners was secure, it was becoming clear that the longer-term threat was serious and, even more worrying, the number of people wanting to emigrate to Australia was also dropping.

However, the citizens of Belfast were not going to let such problems mar Wednesday 16 March 1960, and the city took on a festive air as during the morning thousands of people streamed into the harbour estate by bus, car, bicycle and on foot. Ten thousand lucky ticket-holders were actually admitted to the Musgrave Yard itself, but the launching ceremony could also be watched from a number of vantage points around the yard. During the morning shipyard workers began to hammer away the wooden chocks and shores, and the shipyard foremen anxiously listened to the creaks and groans and watched for any premature movement of the hull. As the morning progressed, work in the shipyard came to a standstill as all the workers who were not engaged in the launch preparations took the opportunity of seeing the product of two and a half years of their labour enter the water.

Few of the VIPs who attended that day were aware that shortly before the launch seven workers who were engaged in making the final preparations had been injured. The accident happened when they were removing heavy wooden props which had been damaged by the great weight of the ship. The men sustained a variety of injuries, including a broken leg, a broken arm and bruises.

Dame Pattie Menzies and other guests had arrived in Liverpool on a special train from London Euston, and it is said that they virtually took over the overnight ferry, *Ulster Prince*, on its night crossing to Belfast. Dame Pattie, who was accompanied by Sir Frederick Rebbeck and Sir William Currie, arrived at the launching platform at 12.15pm, just quarter of an hour before the launch, and the Royal Ulster Constabulary Band struck up Australia's national song 'Waltzing Matilda' to welcome her. Although the rain had stopped during the morning, the day remained overcast, but this did not mar the occasion and Dame Pattie was presented with a bouquet by Harland & Wolff's youngest employee, 17-year-old plater's apprentice, Glenn Carlisle.

The ceremony itself was preceded by a short religious service which was conducted by Rev R. W. Kilpatrick, rector of the shipyard workers' church, St Patrick's, Ballymacarrett. Dame Pattie had brought with her a sprig of white heather taken from a bouquet of flowers which Sir William Currie had had placed in her cabin on the *Arcadia* on sailing day in Sydney, and as a personal gesture she attached this to the launching ribbon which was holding a large bottle of Australian wine, and as the hands of the clock crept round to 12.30pm, all the pre-launch clamour - the ringing sound of the shipwrights' hammers, the music on the loudspeakers, the whistles and shouts of the shipyard workers from their lofty perches among the gantries and cranes and the buzz of conversation from the thousands of assembled guests and spectators - died away. At 'zero hour' an electronically controlled alarm sounded a warning and Dame Pattie named the great ship *Canberra* and pulled a lever which sent the bottle of wine smashing across the bow and at the same time released the triggers of the launching mechanism. Order No 1621, now officially named *Canberra*, moved majestically down slipway 14 and entered the water with a mighty splash and the accompanying clatter of drag chains. Once water-borne the *Canberra* was greeted with the traditional three cheers from the 20,000-strong crowd and by piercing hoots from the sirens of every ship in the harbour. The cheering was led by 82-year-old Sir Frederick Rebbeck, the chairman and managing director of Harland & Wolff, as he had done at every launch from the Belfast yard during the previous 30 years.

Once the new liner had entered the Musgrave Channel a group of six tugs took over. Five of them had been provided by John Cooper Ltd of Belfast and the sixth had come from the Clyde specially for the launch. In command of the *Canberra* was Captain Archie Trace, the Belfast Harbour Board's senior pilot, and with the aid of the six tugs he directed the berthing of the liner at the Thompson Wharf, where her fitting out could begin.

The official luncheon which followed was attended by 300 guests and during the course of the afternoon Sir William Currie spoke of his company's determination to endeavour to keep British shipping supreme. He explained the ideas behind the new Pacific services and how it would be possible to travel round the world in P&O ships, calling at 27 different ports on the way. In a reference to the worrying trend in air travel he said, 'I believe passenger ships will then become convalescent homes for the weary air traveller. Sea travel will offer a real rest from the hectic life of rush - breakfast in London, dinner in New York - or even more rush when and if supersonic air travel becomes a reality.' Although this was still two decades away his ideas were not far off the mark. He then went on to talk about the *Canberra* herself: '...both inside and out the *Canberra* is different in plan and detail from any other ship the company has, but she is not different for the sake of being different. She is only different where we judge we have found some new and better solution to an old problem.'

In her speech Dame Pattie Menzies said that the *Canberra* would be, 'Like a hand of friendship stretching across the sea.' As was customary she was presented with a gift of jewellery, consisting of a set of diamond and sapphire earrings, brooch and bracelet.

It was obviously a moving occasion for Sir Frederick Rebbeck as he told his guests: 'Every time I have driven to the works I have instructed the driver to pass the *Canberra*, and I have watched her rising in the stocks to the huge magnificent vessel she is now.' The Prime Minister of Northern Ireland, Lord Brookeborough, proposed the toast to the *Canberra* and to the P&O Company, and he paid

tribute to the link between the famous shipping company and Harland & Wolff which went back over 80 years. That same night as many of the guests again lined the rails of the *Ulster Prince* for the return crossing to Liverpool, they passed the *Canberra* safely secured alongside her fitting-out berth and once again they gave three hearty cheers.

Throughout the following 12 months work on the vessel carried on apace and by January 1961, with the two funnels having been lifted on board by a floating crane and having been fitted into place, and with much of her superstructure completed, the *Canberra* began to look far more shipshape and by the end of April she was ready to undergo her trials. Captain Michael Bradford, who would himself command the *Canberra* one day, recalls this period when, as the Senior First Officer, he stood by the ship: 'My memories are of endless miles which we seemed to do each day while at her fitting-out berth, walking around and checking this and that, and the feeling of almost total exhaustion at the end of the long day, as there were no lifts to ride from truck to keel, and not always transport to and from the P&O office, situated just opposite Harland & Wolff's main office.'

P&O had appointed as the ship's master Captain Geoffrey Alan Wild, who had already been standing by the *Canberra* since October 1960. Captain Wild was the son of a Lancashire clergyman and he had served his early apprenticeship at the Nautical College, Pangbourne, which he had joined at 14 years of age in 1918. The college had only been formed in 1917 and he had been part of the establishment's second entry of cadets. Following a year at Pangbourne he had spent 12 months as a cadet on the barquentine *St George* and he completed his apprenticeship with the New Zealand Shipping Company which was a P&O subsidiary. He joined the P&O Company in 1923 and he was appointed to the 6,800-ton steamer *Novara* as the Fourth Officer. He obtained his master's certificate in 1929 and during the Second World War he served in a number of the company's ships which had been requisitioned as troop transports. An unusual appointment was as the First Officer in the French liner *Ile de France* which, after the fall of France, was seized in the Far East by the British Government. During the war she was operated by P&O until she was handed back to the French Government in 1944. In that same year Captain Wild went to the USA where, at Baltimore, the P&O liner *Chitral* was undergoing conversion from armed merchant cruiser to troopship by the Maryland Dry Dock Company. The *Chitral* had been in service as one of the Royal Navy's auxiliary cruisers since 1939 and Geoffrey Wild was appointed as her Chief Officer. Following the conversion the *Chitral* served in the Mediterranean and in South-East Asia where, in early September 1945, she took part in the Malayan landings at Morib on the west coast of the peninsula. Fortunately, it was after the Japanese surrender

This view was taken soon after *Canberra* arrived alongside the fitting-out berth and it can be seen that a great deal of work on her superstructure still has to be completed.

(*Belfast Telegraph*)

and the landings were unopposed. In 1949 he was promoted to Staff Captain of the *Stratheden* and following that he commanded the *Canton*, *Corfu*, *Chusan*, *Strathaird*, and the *Arcadia*. He was a very experienced master, but was somewhat surprised by the *Canberra's* futuristic design. Captain Michael Bradford recalls Captain Wild's first visit to the ship and, '...his look of disbelief at finding that there was no ship's wheel and that the mighty vessel was to be steered by a small aircraft steering wheel.'

Captain Michael Prowse was appointed as *Canberra's* first Staff Captain, and like Captain Wild he too had come from serving on the *Arcadia*. He had trained as a *Worcester* cadet prior to starting his apprenticeship with P&O, and his first company appointment was as the Fourth Officer in the *Moldavia*, after which he served in the *Strathaird*, *Maloja*, *Strathmore* and the *Ranchi*, all of which were employed as troopships. After the war he served as the Chief Officer of the *Mooltan*, and subsequently served in the *Iberia* and the *Strathnaver* before joining the *Arcadia* in February 1960.

The *Canberra's* Chief Engineer was Mr John A. Shakle, who had joined the company in 1931, and had served on such venerable old ships as *Naldera*, *Viceroy of India* and the *Carthage*. After the Second World War he served in the *Strathmore* and as the Chief Engineer of the *Iberia*, before being appointed to the *Canberra* in January 1960 and standing by during her construction.

The sheer size and draught of P&O's new liner, and that of the Orient Line's new ship *Oriana*, was such that neither of the two vessels would be able to use Tilbury as their home port and whilst they were under construction a great deal of thought was going into the location of harbour facilities. The most obvious choice was Southampton Docks, whose name had been synonymous with big passenger liners for many years, and as early as February 1959 Sir Brian Robertson, the chairman of the British Transport Commission, had announced that a new passenger terminal which was being built at 106 berth in Southampton's Western Docks, would be used by both the *Canberra* and the *Oriana*. The new terminal would be able to handle 2,000 passengers and their baggage, which both ships would carry on each of their three annual round voyages to Australia and the Pacific. Although the decision to use Southampton meant a considerable loss of trade for London, it was a logical one because by turning round at Southampton a day was cut from the voyage time.

In order to familiarize himself with a ship the size of the *Canberra*, Captain Wild joined the Orient Line's new liner *Oriana* at Naples when she called there on 20 March 1961 during the homeward leg of her maiden voyage. One of the *Oriana's* senior pursers was E. L. (Nelson) French, who sat at the same table as Captain Wild for the four-day passage to Southampton and recalls that, 'Meals were like a radio quiz programme.'

It was just five weeks later, on Saturday 29 April 1961, that the *Canberra* was ready to leave Belfast for the first time to make the short passage down to Southampton. Although Harland & Wolff had built many big passenger liners, and the *Canberra* was some 3,000 tons less than the first White Star liner *Britannic* which had been completed as a hospital ship in 1915, and she and the *Olympic* and *Titanic* were all accommodated in Harland & Wolff's dry dock at Queen's Island, the new P&O liner was just too wide to fit into the Belfast graving dock. It had been arranged, therefore, that the *Canberra* would be docked at Southampton.

For the shipyardmen of Belfast it was a proud but sad occasion and for Harland & Wolff it was a hard blow for, after 20 years with a high level of production, the yard was entering a slump from which it would never fully recover. The *Canberra* had represented the livelihoods of the workers for three and a half years, and for over an hour before she sailed hundreds of men and their families gathered at her berth to watch her leave. As many 'Islandmen' were sailing with the *Canberra* to complete last-minute jobs there was a continuous shouted dialogue between the ship and shore. Shortly after 9.30am, half an hour before departure time, the Prime Minister of Northern Ireland, Lord Brookeborough, arrived with Dr Denis Rebbeck, the deputy managing director of the shipbuilding company. Lord Brookeborough and his wife were spending the day on board the ship and then disembarking in Bangor Bay before *Canberra* left for Southampton.

As 10am approached white smoke billowed from one of the liner's twin funnels and the gangways were swung away. Over the ship's public address system messages and commands could be heard and the Indian seamen in their red turbans lined the forecastle ready to cast off. Three tugs fussed round her stern and at exactly two minutes before ten o' clock the last ropes, and the last links with Belfast, were cast off. As the *Canberra* moved slowly away from her berth and the shell doors slammed shut, a silence came over the watching crowd and as was reported at the time, '... handkerchiefs covered many eyes.' Hundreds of Belfast shipyard workers kept pace with the great liner as she was slowly eased out, stern first, into the Victoria Channel where the tugs swung her bows to face the open sea. Then, at 10.52am, she slowly moved into Belfast Lough where the black smoke from the tugs and the fog which was hanging over Belfast almost obliterated her from view. Meanwhile, on shore, traffic on the Sydenham Bypass came to a standstill as motorists stopped for a grandstand view of the great white liner. At Holywood the traffic congestion was reported by the AA to be worse than on any Bank Holiday as the *Canberra* made her way out of her birthplace.

Although the port had been closed to both inward and outward shipping whilst the *Canberra* made her way to the open sea, it did not stop a fleet of small boats following her past the fog-shrouded and almost invisible Bangor coastline. Finally, when the last tug slipped her line, the *Canberra* was on her own, under her own power for the first time.

On the bridge Captain Wild was in command but, as the ship had not been formally handed over to P&O, he was accompanied by Belfast's senior pilot, Captain Archie Trace and his assistant, Captain John Mclarnon. Another who was on the bridge that day was the deputy managing director of Harland & Wolff, Dr Denis Rebbeck, who recalled the event thus: 'It was not without a feeling of nostalgia that I stood on the bridge of the *Canberra* as she slowly pulled away from her fitting-out berth on Saturday 29 April, and I watched the faces of the hundreds of workmen who were saying their final farewell to a ship that had become part of themselves over four and a half years. Queen's Island and, synonymously, the city of Belfast had taken a real pride in the construction of this the largest passenger ship built in the United Kingdom since the days of the *Queens*, and those of us most intimately connected with the challenging task of building this wonderful liner felt that the task had been faithfully carried out in the spirit of fullest co-operation which had been urged upon us all.'v

One of the liner's great funnels is about to be lifted on board, while the other funnel still sits on the dockside waiting its turn to be fitted. *(Ulster Folk & Transport Museum)*

Chapter Three

Every Ship Is An Individual

The *Canberra* was not the first passenger liner to be designed with her main propulsion machinery placed aft, for both the Shaw Savill liner of 1955, *Southern Cross*, (which is still in service as the *Ocean Breeze*), and the Dutch liner *Rotterdam* of 1959, were built to this design. However, neither of these two ships was as big or as powerful as the *Canberra* and a great deal of design work was required on the part of both the owners and the builders in order to get everything absolutely right. In fact, the *Southern Cross* had been built by Harland & Wolff at Belfast and there is no doubt that the experience gained would stand them in good stead when it came to the construction of the *Canberra*.

The design of the *Canberra* was the brainchild of P&O's gifted naval architect John West who, in the mid-1950s, was appointed as the Assistant General Manager of the company's team which was to design and oversee the building of the liner. In simple terms he was asked to design a ship of between 40,000 and 45,000 gross tons, with a passenger capacity of over 2,000, and with accommodation of a high standard. Right from the start John West decided that the main propulsion machinery would be placed aft for, in the orthodox layout, the machinery occupied the central section of the ship which divided the public passenger spaces and imposed a rigid pattern into which the detailed design had to fit. As well as placing the machinery aft there would be no hatches to the cargo holds, and funnels and masts would be reduced to a bare minimum. In the words of John West, 'In designing the *Canberra* the accent was on passengers.'

Although Shaw Savill's *Southern Cross* had led the way during the 1950s by being a one-class ship, P&O was not yet ready to drop the class barriers and so the *Canberra* was designed to carry both first and tourist class passengers. The interior planning of the vessel was co-ordinated by Sir Hugh Casson in association with McInnes, Gardner & Partners. Assisted by Timothy Rendall, he designed the cinema and all the first class public rooms except the Crow's Nest. The tourist class public rooms and the Crow's Nest were the work of John Wright and Frederick Hickman, while Miss Barbara Oakley was responsible for the interiors of cabins, crew's quarters and adjoining alleyways and courts. Sir Hugh Casson loved ships and particularly passenger liners and he had an affinity with the vessels of the P&O because, in the early years of the 20th century, his parents had first met on board a P&O liner during a voyage between London and Bombay. He set out five main principles to guide him and his team which, in

his own words, '..helped to keep us afloat' and it is worth quoting them here:-

1) The smallest detail counts, and only the best is worth aiming at.

2) The sea, a magical and constantly changing background, is there. So too, are the dramatic, even bizarre, shapes and lines of naval architecture. They should be used, not hidden away.

3) Every ship is an individual with a distinct personality. A designer cannot create this, but he can help to form it and avoid stifling it with characterless treatments that might be found on any deck in any ship.

4) A ship has a long life. It is not done over every year like a shoe shop or a coffee bar. While it is not possible to ignore fashion, it is important not to become its prisoner. There is nothing more dowdy than last year's dernier cri.

5) Ship interiors demand simple forms, clean surfaces, clear colours and good materials left to speak for themselves. Sprinklers and air-conditioning are necessary, but we do not want them pressed on our attention. Upholstery and carpets must obviously be able to take a reasonable amount of dirt and staining, but there is no need to use patterns that look dirty (and therefore disgusting) when new.

A measure of the difficulties faced by the designers was summed up by Sir Hugh Casson when he observed that, 'A successful interior must therefore look as cosy in Tilbury Docks in February as it looks cool and fresh in the Red Sea.'

The accommodation for *Canberra's* 548 first class passengers was, like most two-class ships, situated amidships and it occupied eight decks from the Sun Deck down to E Deck. The first class public rooms included the Pacific Restaurant, a lounge called the Meridian Room, the Menzies Room for reading and writing, and a private room for dining or entertaining called the Crystal Room. There was also an observation lounge called the Crow's Nest, the Bonito Club which was the ballroom, and a children's playroom. The cinema was open to both first and tourist class passengers.

The tourist class accommodation catered for 1,690 passengers and was situated aft of the first class section on ten decks from the Sun Deck down to G Deck. The tourist class public rooms included a lounge called the William Fawcett Room, reading rooms and a library, the main bar which was named the Cricketers' Tavern, a smoking room called the Peacock Room, and the Alice Springs Room which was the poolside café. The dance floor was in the Island Room and there was a room for

The first class Crow's Nest was the observation lounge where the large picture windows overlooked the forecastle. The deck was laid in teak, with the forward area carpeted in black with white, lemon, gold and brown motifs. Among the room's many interesting features were the scale model navigation buoys, one of which can be seen in the photograph.   *(P&O)*

Aft of the stadium games area and the main first class foyer and staircase was the Bonito Club. This view shows the central dance floor with the sliding glass bulkhead in the background opened out onto the swimming pool.   *(P&O)*

Looking forward from the Bonito Pool one can see the terracing of the *Canberra's* superstructure and the warmth of the Bonito Club. *(P&O)*

The main first class lounge, the Meridian Room, was situated at the forward end of the Promenade Deck. The main central seating area of the lounge was illuminated by a spiky and angular ceiling light some 30ft long which was made up of glittering metal facets.

(P&O)

teenagers which went by the name of the Pop Inn. The tourist class dining saloon was the Atlantic Restaurant and at the time it was thought to be the largest restaurant afloat.

The uppermost deck for both classes was the Sun Deck, with the midship section being reserved for first class passengers. This area was situated aft of the terraced bridge superstructure and it looked down onto the deck below where there was a terraced recess enclosing the first class swimming pool. The bridge superstructure provided protection from the wind off the sea while the terracing gave the whole area a spacious feel and this was enhanced by the open deck spaces forward of the funnels. Large glass screens on both the port and starboard sides extended right aft to the area abaft the funnel casings and provided excellent protection from the elements.

Below the Sun Deck came the Games Deck where the observation lounge, the Crow's Nest, overlooked the forecastle. Situated as it was within the sweeping curve of

the forward bulkhead, its 41 full-height windows afforded magnificent views out over the bows. There were also large picture windows in the after section which looked out onto the Stadium Deck, a games area within an open well. There were three entrances into the Crow's Nest, one from both the port and starboard sides of the Sun Deck, while the third was a large spiral staircase which rose up through three decks from the main lounge on the Promenade Deck and terminated in the centre of the room. All the wall surfaces here were flush and painted in eggshell white as were the deckheads, which were close boarded in the style of a yacht, with concealed lighting. The deck was laid in teak, with the forward area carpeted in black with white, lemon, gold and brown motifs. Roller blinds were fitted to all the windows for screening at night and these were made up of thin wooden slats woven into a coloured cotton backing. On the port and starboard sides of the after bulkhead two large, rectangular screens concealed the bar and pantry areas, and they displayed feature maps in relief of Southampton Water

From the Meridian Room a large spiral staircase rose up through three decks and terminated in the Crow's Nest. This dramatic shot shows the Meridian Room from the base of the staircase. *(P&O)*

One of the *Canberra's* first class two- or three-berth staterooms, where the third berth converted for daytime use as a settee. *(P&O)*

A splendid view looking forward along the first class section of the Sun Deck at the terraced superstructure. *(P&O)*

and the Solent, and Sydney Harbour. These were fitted with small, illuminated marker buoys which indicated the shipping channels of both ports. Other interesting features of the room were the scale model navigation buoys and a magnetic repeater compass. This was situated forward of the staircrase balustrade and as it was linked to the ship's main compass it gave an accurate recording of the ship's course. The furniture throughout the room had a typical 1960s spindly look and the chairs were based on a contemporary 'Bertoia' design in a chromium-plated wire basket construction, upholstered in yellow and white tweeds. There were also matching stools and occasional tables with white plastic tops and satin chrome underframes.

Aft of the stadium games area and the main first class

foyer and staircase was the Bonito Club, which originally was to have been named the Abolido Club, and it was designed so that as far as possible, the swimming pool and its terracing would appear to be one space. The teak decking of the pool terrace was extended into the centre of the café to form the dance floor and the whole of the glass bulkhead, which was the only division between the terracing and the café, could slide vertically into the deck to form one continuous deck surface so that dancing could continue outside. The dance area was lit by soft, golden diffused lighting which shone down through honeycomb shaped openings in the glass-reinforced plastic deckhead. The café tables at either side of the room were illuminated internally and gave a soft glow through their decorative top surfaces which were in fibreglass and decorated with painted designs based on Aboriginal symbols and traditional drawings. The orchestra was spotlighted against a dark, richly-coloured mural decoration. The swimming pool was tiled in white mosaic and was set within the enclosing tiers of terraces which formed a sheltered arena.

The main first class lounge, the Meridian Room, was situated three decks down at the forward end of the Promenade Deck. In planning the lounge area, several smaller and related spaces, such as a sit-up bar, writing rooms, library and service rooms were required, as well as the large spiral staircrase which ascended to the Crow's Nest. The chief feature of the design was an open-plan arrangement, with the whole area being designed virtually as one room. By using a series of curving bulkheads, smaller areas for seating were formed within the 'folds'. The central staircase rose up as a brightly lit spiral inside one of these dark panelled folds. At the forward end of the room the curving bulkheads enclosed the sit-up Century Bar, the counter of which was designed as a sculptural shape formed by laminations of dark hardwood. In contrast to the curving screen bulkheads, the main central seating area of the lounge was illuminated by a spiky and angular ceiling light some 30ft long which was made up of glittering metal facets. The decorative effect in the lounge was obtained mainly from the lounge chairs which were specially designed in glass-reinforced plastic. Brightly coloured removable covers fitted over the foam-upholstered plastic shells, which created a light, nautical appearance and showed a clear departure from the tradition of the 'club' armchairs which were previously found in ships' lounges.

In the main foyer on the Promenade Deck there was hung a delicate line and watercolour portrait of Dame Pattie Menzies GBE, by the artist John Stanton Ward ARA, while around the forward landings there were a number of decorative inlays by the painter and etcher Julian Otto Trevelyan, depicting the four continents of America, Africa, India and Australia.

Aft of the Meridian Room and the main entrance foyer, on the starboard side of the ship, was the Crystal Room which was used for private parties. The walls of this room were of a light grey wood veneer in parquet strips, while the deckhead was covered with a white plastic, louvred grid

The purpose-built cinema on board the *Canberra* was used by both first and tourist class passengers with separate entrances for each class. *(P&O)*

which was illuminated to give an overall diffused lighting effect, and which could be adjusted by means of a dimmer switch. The carpet in the room was a dark, mottled leaf green and black, with the surrounding edging in white terrazzo. The satin chrome tables had reversible tops which were baize on one side and black leather on the other, and to complement them the glass-reinforced plastic and satin chrome chairs were covered in bright orange fabric. The focal point of the room was a decorative panel in resin and glass fragments which was used as a setting for small botanical specimens.

The first class children's playroom was on the starboard side of the Games Deck, situated amidships, just forward of the tourist class ballroom. The room was mainly pale blue in colour with a blue rubber deck covering, and the bulkheads were decorated with a mural of children at play and famous characters from children's books, all in the soft drawing and colouring style of the artist Edward J. I. Ardizzone who, in 1956, had been honoured as the Library Association's best illustrator of children's books. Apart from the usual toys in the playroom there was a Wendy House and a 'rocket' into which the children could climb and view the deck above through a periscope. The forward half of the room could be opened up when weather conditions permitted to give access to an outside deck space.

The first class restaurant was on E deck and it was situated forward of the main staircase and foyer. The chief aim when designing the Pacific Restaurant was to counteract the uncongenial effect that a very large area can

In the tourist section of the ship the central meeting point for passengers was the main lounge, the William Fawcett Room, on the Promenade Deck. It was designed on the lines of a 'Palm Court', complete with fountains where bubbling fluorescent water surged and spiralled upwards in pipes inside a glass tank. The furniture was modelled in bent plywood, veneered in black bean and upholstered in bronzed green leather. However, the fountains were a problem once at sea and they were removed after the vessel's initial trials.

(P&O)

Right aft on the Promenade Deck was the tourist class Peacock Room, which was designed specifically to provide a quiet atmosphere for smoking and reading. The canopy over the central dance floor was removed following the vessel's trials. *(P&O)*

The Alice Springs Room was conspicuous for its cane furniture and decor of glass mosaics. The sliding glass doors opened out onto the after swimming pool. *(P&O)*

The tourist class ballroom, the Island Room, was situated on the Games Deck and during the day the compartment was used for concerts and games. In hot weather it was possible to open up both sides, and the port side also doubled as a playground for children from the tourist class playroom. *(P&O)*

produce, as the compartment extended over the full width of the ship with a relatively low ceiling height. Because E Deck was too low down in the ship to allow portholes to be fitted, an artificial lighting scheme was needed which would make the restaurant bright and cheerful and offset any feeling of oppression which the lack of natural light might create. The first problem of the room size was solved by raising a portion of the ceiling, by having a sunken area in the centre of the deck which was reached by steps, and by using pillar casings to form screen walls which prevented the whole of the room being visible from any one point. Additional visual dividers were designed in the form of high-backed banquette seating in bays on either side of the ship, each bay accommodating 12 passengers and forming, as it were, small rooms on their own. It was considered essential that the clear lighting required for breakfast and lunch should be subdued and of a different style for dinner in the evening. During the day there were bright ceiling lights, clusters of glowing cylinders specially woven from fibreglass and running continuously on both sides of the

room, and the light they produced was filtered through woven screens to give the effect of strong sunlight. At night this lighting was replaced by glowing lanterns which were placed in the centre of each table to create a more sophisticated atmosphere. The room was finished in natural wood and leather and the deck was carpeted throughout. An inlay was worked as a frieze into the wooden balustrade around the central lower section, and an inlaid relief formed the main feature on the bulkhead behind the captain's table. The restaurant had a Polynesian theme with motifs of bone, shell and metal set into the wood panelling, while the decoration was dominated by a full-size replica of a war canoe which was the work of Harold Gower at the British Museum.

Throughout *Canberra's* first class section the passageway bulkheads were white relieved with black, eggshell blue and straw yellow. The rubber flooring was in a deep Mediterranean blue and black which provided continuity without monotony. All the deckheads were flush with lights recessed above them. The bulkheads in the first class cabins

The tourist class Atlantic Restaurant was situated on E Deck and it could accommodate 704 passengers at one sitting. Outboard the seating on each side was divided by free-shaped fins which formed bays in a layout which was designed to prevent the impression of being in a canteen while, at the same time, retaining the vista across the vast compartment through the cutaway central sections of the fins. *(P&O)*

were covered in a soft plastic, with a linen texture and finished in easily cleaned, moisture-resistant surfaces. A large amount of white was used and with dark, close-fitted charcoal carpets and simple grained woods of deep colours with occasional bright highlights, passengers were provided with surroundings that were restful without being dull.

The largest proportion of first class accommodation was arranged in groups looking onto courts which had three large windows in the ship's side. Each room had a control panel for radio, temperature control, two-way light switches and service telephones. In the first class shower cabins the dressing table, writing table and a small chest of drawers were fitted to give a continuous top surface which linked them together and gave them a tailor-made appearance. For passengers who wanted more space and added luxury, there were four veranda suites and eight de

luxe cabins situated amidships on C Deck; two of the suites and four of the de luxe cabins had communicating doors. Four different colour schemes were used in these staterooms to complement the furniture of teak, Swedish pine, elm and rosewood. Each of the de luxe cabins had a folding bed, a bed settee, a writing table, a double wardrobe, a dressing table and a bedside table which housed the lighting, air-conditioning and ventilation controls, telephone and radio. The main item of furniture in both the suites and the de luxe cabins was a unit which housed a refrigerator, clock, radio, 17-inch television set and a cocktail cabinet. There were also two easy chairs, as well as a settee, a writing chair and a dressing stool. All 12 suites had four large picture windows and all were completely soundproofed.

None of the first class cabins normally accommodated

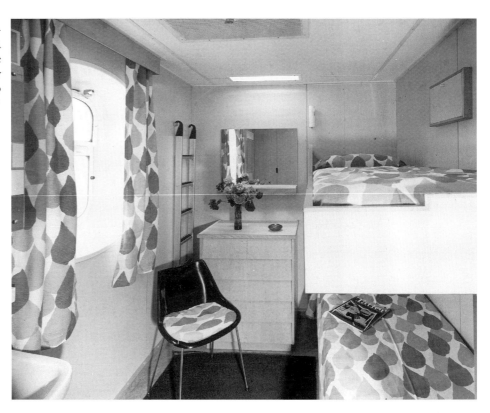

A comfortable outside two-berth tourist class cabin on A Deck. During the day the upper berth could fold away allowing the lower bunk to be used as a settee. *(P&O)*

more than two passengers, although a few on C and D Decks could be converted for the use of three. As would be expected, all the first class cabins were fitted with bathrooms or showers, and WC facilities.

In the tourist class section of the ship the central meeting point for passengers was the main lounge, the William Fawcett Room, on the Promenade Deck. Because the ship carried almost 1,700 passengers in this class, it was a very large room and was flanked on either side aft, by writing rooms and a library. The lounge itself was designed on the lines of a 'Palm Court', complete with fountains and a considerable area covered in mirrors. The outer bulkheads were of a silver-white fibreglass, and cutting in at right angles were screens embellished with tinted mirror-glass murals, designed by Professor Robert Y. Goodden CBE of the School of Silversmithing and Jewellery. Two much larger screens, set in black beanwood, faced each other in the centre of the room, where they ran fore and aft. A central feature in the lounge was made up of two fountains where bubbling fluorescent water surged and spiralled upwards in pipes inside a glass tank. Small balls were then caught and tossed by the water to provide a continuous dancing effect, which was intended to enhance the 'Palm Court' atmosphere. The furniture here was modelled in bent plywood, veneered in black bean and upholstered in bronzed green leather and pure silk tweed in purple

patterns. The curtains were in alternate blocks of greyish mauve and pink, and the carpet was a deep gold colour.

Aft of the William Fawcett Room, on the starboard side of the ship, was the Pop Inn which was designed for teenagers along the lines of a late 1950s coffee bar. It was equipped with a jukebox and there was ample room for dancing and games such as table tennis. The wooden bulkheads were of deal into which pokerwork designs had been burnt, and there were also paintings by students of the Royal College of Art, including the 23-year-old David Hockney. The bar tops were made up of bands of coloured perspex placed against each other and interspersed with fluorescent strips, and nylon 'fur' fabric was used for the furniture upholstery. The room was lit by a continuous multicoloured, irregular shaped light fitting on the deckhead, and at the after end of the Pop Inn there was a small sitting room with drink-dispensing machines.

Aft of the William Fawcett Room, on the port side of the ship, was the main tourist class bar, the Cricketers' Tavern, which incorporated the atmosphere of an English 'pub' with the game of cricket as its theme. The famous England cricketer Colin Cowdrey was, in fact, asked to act as a consultant, and the long narrow room, divided down its length by groups of individual tables with semi-circular seating, was decorated with a montage of bats, balls, caps, pads, gloves and stumps. Projecting at right angles on the

Attended by the tugs *Dunnose* and *Formby*, the *Canberra* leaves Southampton for her maiden voyage to Australia. She is flying the P&O house-flag at her masthead and the Royal Mail pennant at the truck.

(Beken of Cowes)

outboard bulkhead were screens with life-size portraits by Ruskin Spear RA of W. G. Grace, Sir Donald Bradman, Learie Constantine and K. S. Ranjitsinhije. Behind the bar, which was of willow and white marble, was a display of nearly 200 ties representing famous cricket clubs, while the wooden handhold at the front of the bar was wound round with black twine in the manner of a cricket bat handle.

Right aft on the Promenade Deck was the tourist class Peacock Room, which was designed specifically to provide a quiet atmosphere for smoking and reading. At

The starboard side of the tourist class Games Deck was a pleasant sheltered area which would later be enclosed by windbreaks. *(Neil McCart)*

the after end there were two adjoining rooms which were intended as card-playing and games rooms. A small area of the floor could be cleared in the evenings for dancing and there was a waiter service bar. The bulkheads were covered in a dyed blue wood veneer, with the same decoration being used for the deckhead as well. When the curtains were drawn they formed a continuous drape around the sides, the fabric design being stripes with orange and gold and a peacock motif. The furniture was all made from bent pine plywood and covered in leather, and some of the large easy chairs were joined together to form a sofa. The deck covering was white, with the dance floor marked out in diagonal black stripes, while there was carpeting in the card rooms. Over the central part of the Peacock Room hung a canopy which was designed by Mr R. Adams, who also created the bas-relief mural opposite the bar counter.

There were two swimming pools in the tourist class section, one of which, at the after end of B Deck, was called the Alice Springs and featured an undercover café-bar. The second pool, at the after end of the Games Deck, was called the Lido and here there was a toddlers' paddling pool as well. The Alice Springs Room was conspicuous for its decor of glass mosaics in multicoloured feather-like designs by the sculptor Arnold Machin RA. Cane furniture was chosen for this room and the same material was used on the bar front.

The tourist class ballroom, the Island Room, was also situated on the Games Deck and during the day the compartment was used for concerts and games. In hot weather it was possible to open up both sides, and the port

side of the room also doubled as a playground for children from the tourist class playroom. All around the inner bulkhead was a vast and immensely colourful mural, which was laminated into the wall panels. It featured Ceylon (Sri Lanka) and the Pacific Islands and was the work of Mr Robert Buhler RA. The furniture in the room was laid out in 'islands' on white Indian rugs, and the tables and four different chair designs were cut from laminated plywood.

The tourist class playroom was situated forward of the Island Room on the port side of the ship, and it was an airy room in which the basic colour scheme was white and yellow. Laminated into the white plastic walls was a mural of imaginary birds and animals by Mary Feddon and this ran along both ends of the room and in a semi-circle behind the carousel which was worked by the children themselves riding small bicycles. There was also a Wendy House, a wheelhouse and a slide, together with the traditional rocking horse and doll's pram. At certain times of the day the children had the use of a section of the Island Room as a playground.

The tourist class Atlantic Restaurant was on E Deck, aft of the galley and food preparation rooms, and it could accommodate 704 passengers at one sitting. Outboard, the seating on each side was divided by free-shaped fins which formed bays in a layout that was designed to prevent the impression of being in a canteen while, at the same time, retaining the vista across the vast compartment through the cutaway central sections of the fins. The shape of the room was accentuated at night by the white ceiling which described a parabolic curve almost to the outer edges where there was a margin of darkness. The centre of the ceiling was of brightly lit white fibreglass and there was a two-way control on the lighting so that it could be softened for dining at night. The bulkheads were of iridescent green-gold fibreglass and the deck was dark blue, with the plywood furniture being upholstered in dark blue and khaki leather. At the main entrance and in each bay there were green metal sculptures by Mr Geoffrey Clarke, who had also designed relief sculptures for the *Oriana*.

All the tourist class cabins, which were two- and four-berth rooms, had foldaway upper berths, which left a maximum of clear space available during the day. There were also blocks of tourist class cabins which could be used as four-berth rooms, or as two-berth cabins complete with a shower and WC. All the tourist class cabins had plastic bulkheads in pale colours, with simple beech furniture. Some cabins had soft grey bulkheads with bedspreads and curtains printed in a bright pink and tangerine design, while others had pale blue bulkheads with white, blue and green soft furnishings.

To add to passenger comfort the whole of the first and tourist class accommodation was air-conditioned, as was most of the officers' and crew accommodation. To ensure that all these areas were served the *Canberra* was fitted with one of the largest marine air-conditioning installations ever designed, with 17 miles of air ducts, through which the fans moved the equivalent of 50 tons of air each day. All the passenger cabins had individual temperature controls and, as a further improvement, specially designed sound-resistant cabin bulkheads were fitted throughout the passenger spaces.

The captain and his senior officers were accommodated on three decks within the terraced bridge superstructure and, as they had a considerable amount of entertaining to do as part of their duties, their cabins all had individual colour schemes with furniture designed to give a light effect. Refrigerators and television sets were included in fitted units of bookshelves, cupboards and drawers. Junior officers each had their own cabin and the officers' smoking room at the after end of the Games Deck, overlooking the first class games area, was panelled in larch with full-length midnight-blue and navy-blue check curtains along one side of the room. For the petty officers, leading hands and other European crew members, there were two recreation rooms at the forward end of C Deck and these were fitted with cool-coloured plastic bulkheads. The European stewards had a mess room amidships, on the port side of F Deck, and this compartment was decorated in pale grey, black and red. Arrangements of green plants in pots and tubs helped to break up the straight lines of the tables and chairs, and transparent fibreglass screens decorated with abstract designs ran along the length of the outboard side.

As was the custom on all P&O passenger ships a large number of crew members came from India with the great majority of stewards being recruited from the former Portuguese colony of Goa. The historical significance of this was that in return for its help to the royalist cause during the Iberian Wars of the 1880s, P&O was awarded a charter allowing it to employ subjects of Goa as servants, and of the 800 crew members on *Canberra* about 315 were Goans. The senior Goan was the Assistant Accommodation Supervisor, and under him 66 men were employed in the food preparation rooms, over 107 as waiters in the restaurants, 42 as cabin stewards and more than 20 in the laundry. The rest were employed on general cleaning duties and helping to maintain the hotel services. The Goans had a large recreation and mess room on the port side of F Deck, forward of the European stewards' mess. The background colour on the plastic bulkheads was grey, and the recreation area was furnished with bookcases, writing tables and an altar, all veneered in straight-grained elm. The Goanese, having been converted by Portuguese missionaries in the 15th century, were all devout Roman Catholics and so an altar was always included in their recreation room on P&O ships.

To cater for the appetites of over 3,000 people the *Canberra* was fitted with a large, well-equipped main galley amidships on E Deck, between the two passenger restaurants. It was 150 feet long and extended over the full width of the ship. Situated directly beneath the galley, and connected to it by lifts, were the fish-preparing room, the bakery and the butcher's shop, while the confectionery shop and the cold pantries were within the main kitchen area. In order to prepare morning tea and light snacks, service pantries were arranged on all decks, each one equipped with tea-brewing machines and coffee-making equipment.

The *Canberra* was also equipped with a full-size laundry, as well as a number of small self-service launderettes which were sited on most decks in both the first and tourist class sections. These were available for passengers who preferred to do their own laundry and there were washing machines and spin-dryers as well as airing and ironing facilities.

There were five passenger lifts on the ship. The two in the first class were situated in the main foyer where one served E Deck to the Captain's Deck, while the other connected E Deck to the Sun Deck. Two of those in the tourist section were in the main tourist class foyer and they served F Deck to the Games Deck. Finally there was a third lift for the tourist class, situated further aft on the port side and serving D to A Decks.

Originally it was intended that the *Canberra* would carry various types of cargo in addition to passengers' baggage and even their cars but, if conventional cargo holds and hatches had been fitted, it would have imposed serious limitations on the design of the ship's superstructure. With cargo hatches trunked through a number of decks, a considerable amount of passenger accommodation would

A fine aerial view of the *Canberra's* midship section showing her terraced superstructure and the first class Bonito Pool area.

(FotoFlite)

When in her home port of Southampton the *Canberra* normally tied up at 106 berth in the Western Docks, but in this 1970s view she is alongside the port's Ocean Terminal which was usually associated with the great Cunarders. *(Neil McCart)*

Sydney was always regarded as the *Canberra's* second home. Here she is shown alongside the port's Overseas Passenger Terminal. *(D. Stevens)*

have been lost and so it was decided to install special transporters to operate through the ship's side. Two transporters were fitted forward which consisted of a steel boom, carried on rollers within the vessel and power driven to extend 30 feet from the side of the ship. Both were fitted with a travelling carriage, which carried the operator, and from which was suspended a hoist with a cargo platform. When loading or unloading, the doors were opened in the ship's side and the boom was traversed outwards over the dockside where the car or container could be loaded onto the cargo platform and hoisted inboard. In the event the proposal that the *Canberra* should carry cargo was abandoned with the result that she would then be 'stern heavy', a problem which was overcome initially by loading tons of ballast in the form of pig-iron. Later in her career, however, the holds were converted to bunkers and tanks, and the pig-iron ballast was dispensed with.

In order to deal quickly with the thousands of items of baggage which would be carried on each voyage, an integral conveyor system was built in which could move the luggage between the baggage rooms and any of the passenger decks. It could also be loaded on board and unloaded by means of a baggage room conveyor which ran from shell doors on E Deck through to the baggage room on F Deck, or to the elevator which served the passenger decks.

One of the most important decisions which had to be made prior to work starting on the ship's construction concerned the choice of main propulsion machinery, and extensive design studies were undertaken on behalf of P&O by the Yarrow-Admiralty Research Department. Finally it was decided that the *Canberra* would be a twin-screw ship driven by turbo-electric machinery which developed 85,000 SHP to give her a service speed of 27$\frac{1}{2}$ knots. Although there has been more powerful shipboard turbo-electric machinery, the *Canberra's* was the most powerful British-built installation and there is no doubt that it proved extremely successful.

As has previously been described the engines were placed aft, which was a radical move for such a large vessel, but the precedent for turbo-electric machinery had been set in 1928 with the company's *Viceroy of India* and followed two years later with the *Strathnaver* and *Strathaird*. There were a number of distinct advantages in choosing this type of machinery and its position in the ship. Not only did it allow for improved passenger accommodation, but it provided a much greater flexibility in the arrangement. The boilers could be arranged above and aft of the propeller motors, allowing for short runs of steam piping to the turbo-alternators which were forward of the propulsion motors. At the time the three Foster Wheeler ESD type boilers were the largest steam raising units to be fitted in a British ship, and were built under licence by Harland & Wolff. The three main boilers generated superheated steam at 750psi and at a temperature of 960°F for two British

Thomson-Houston (BT-H) turbo-alternators, and these in turn supplied the power to two 42-pole synchronous propeller motors. As well as the flexibility already referred to, the propeller motors could be powered by one turbo-alternator to achieve economical cruising. This was to prove an important factor in helping to save the *Canberra* from an early demise at the hands of the shipbreakers when her original role as a passenger liner came to a premature end as a result of airline competition and sudden and very steep increases in the price of fuel oil.

Probably of greater interest to the passengers than all these technical facts were the Denny-Brown activated-fin stabilizers. These two aerofoil-shaped fins were fitted on both sides of the underwater hull and when required they could be extended and then oscillated synchronously to create a righting movement which opposed the roll of the ship when under way. Another point of interest concerned the bow propellers which were mounted in an athwartship tunnel about 70 feet from the ship's bow, and which proved to be of considerable assistance when manoeuvring alongside in docks around the world.

Originally the *Canberra* had 24 lifeboats which could carry a total of 3,362 people, and all of them were fully equipped with emergency rations including food and water, torches and knives. All but two of the boats were 36 feet long with a seating capacity for 144. Six of these were powered by marine diesel and they were also designed to be used for ship to shore services in ports at which the *Canberra* had to anchor offshore, while the other 16 were fitted with hand propelling gear which had proved to be both sturdy and reliable. The remaining two boats were 26 ft, combined rescue/accident motor lifeboats, each fitted with a fully equipped radio cabin and able to carry 25 people.

That the *Canberra* was very different from any other ship which P&O had ever owned is highlighted by one of the company's senior employees who described his first impressions of her: 'Once aboard I became bewildered for *Canberra* did not conform to the usual layout of P&O ships, and with work still to be done in the way of labelling and numbering, I took 15 minutes to find my cabin. With the engines further aft, the great central section of the ship is given over to cabins; gone are the long, white painted alleyways, and corridors have a habit of turning off at right angles. With a ship 100 feet wide this may have been inevitable. The court cabins are fascinating. The main alleyway goes down the centre of the ship and from it "courts" or minor alleyways branch out and to one's surprise the sea can be seen. The innermost cabins have a window looking out on the sea, the corridor widening with each pair of cabins, where the window is inserted, until at the end there is a wide space, or court, with a settee and gaily coloured cushions. The cabins themselves have settees and look like charming little sitting rooms during the day.

The most remarkable view is from the bridge; when looking aft, one sees an amazing expanse of sun decks below, both first and tourist, with glass screens along the sides. Below is the first class swimming pool, well sheltered for sunbathers. Below the Sun Deck is the Games Deck, where right forward under the bridge is the Crow's Nest, looking down to the sea from a great height and corresponding to the observation lounges in the *Arcadia* and *Iberia*. It is furnished with easy chairs of a modern and unusual design, but which are nonetheless extremely comfortable. An ornamental spiral staircase takes one down to A Deck. Adjoining the Crow's Nest is the Stadium, an enclosed space for sports and competitions with seats all around and which can be covered over if desired. Further aft is the Bonito Club with a dance floor surrounded by tables and looking out upon the swimming pool.

On decks A and B are cabins, mostly of the court type, but the Promenade Deck below them has public rooms throughout its length, with a considerable open promenade almost around the ship. In the centre is the Bureau with a bank, a travel bureau and letter bureau. Then there is a writing room and library, the shop and finally the Meridian Room which, with its dark panelling and heavily curtained windows, seems designed more for winter travel. I liked particularly the restaurant on E Deck with its centre floor lower and its outside tables somewhat higher. One can see almost everyone in the room in this way and the table lighting is most effective as is the lighting from the sides, giving a sunlike glow throughout.

Tourist class passengers will find themselves in a standard of comfort which maintains the trend remarked upon in *Oriana*. The designers have kept in mind that there will be nearly 1,700 passengers to cater for, and on walking round their quarters I could see how this has been planned. They share the spacious Sun Deck with the first class as well as the after part of the Games Deck. A and B Decks, from amidships aft are filled with cabins, all fitted with hot and cold running water, as well as an ice-water tap and a radio, under individual control. Many B Deck cabins amidships are convertible from four to two berths and have a private shower and WC. On A deck are the shop and the hairdressing salon.

The tourist passengers have their own Purser as well as a bank and travel bureau. Next comes the pleasant William Fawcett Room, named after the Peninsular Company's first ship - a model of which will be found there. Going aft again you will see, on the port side, the Cricketers' Tavern, its walls lined with bats autographed by test teams. On the starboard side is the Pop Inn which, as a self-acknowledged "square" I entered with some trepidation. Here a jukebox gave out tunes beloved of the teenager, and nearby was a cold drinks machine, which for sixpence (2$^{1}/_{2}$p), offered sparkling or still drinks in limeade, kola, cherryade and orangeade. The walls are lined with what I believe are "hep cat" expressions and slogans. Further aft is the Peacock Room with a television in the corner for those seeking additional entertainment. Cabin accommodation continues on C, D, E and F Decks, with a smaller number on G Deck.

I spent some time in the engine room and I wish some of our former engineers could have been there. It was cool and lofty, and when we were making nearly 30 knots the vibration was almost non-existent.'

There is no doubt that, in the early summer of 1961, the *Canberra* was most accurately described by *The Times* newspaper as 'A Ship That Shapes The Future'.

An aerial view of the after section of the ship showing the tourist class Lido Pool with the toddlers' paddling pool, which were on the Games Deck, and the Alice Springs Pool which was right aft on B Deck.

(FotoFlite)

A scale profile drawing of the *Canberra* as she appeared on completion.

(*John Bowen*)

The final lines are cast off as a pristine *Canberra* makes her departure from Harland & Wolff's shipyard on Saturday 29 April 1961.

(Ulster Folk & Transport Museum)

Chapter Four

Maiden Voyage

After leaving her fitting-out berth at Belfast the *Canberra* stayed in Belfast Lough to carry out anchor trials, compass adjustments, radar calibration and bow propeller tests, before leaving for the open sea on the evening of Saturday 29 April 1961. During her voyage to Southampton she carried out engine manoeuvring and vibration trials as well as fuel consumption trials and at dawn on the morning of Monday 1 May she arrived off the Nab Tower for her first passage through the Solent and into Southampton Water where, still flying the Harland & Wolff house-flag, she was a magnificent sight for the morning commuters who travelled between Hythe and the city. However, instead of going alongside 106 berth she was manoeuvred up the River Test to No 7 dry dock, the King George V Graving Dock where, at 9.07am, the first lines went out to the dockhead and she was berthed without any problems whatsoever. She was to spend nine days in the dry dock during which time her underwater hull would be examined and cleaned and the final stages of the fitting out would be completed.

The crew of the tug *Carrickfergus* look on as the *Canberra* leaves Belfast for the misty waters of Belfast Lough and dry docking at Southampton.   *(FotoFlite)*

Soon after her arrival the press interviewed Captain Wild, who said that he had been very pleased with the ship's behaviour on her first sea passage, particularly from the navigating point of view, commenting that, 'I was very pleased with the vessel's performance in handling and I think that with her hull form she is going to be a sea kindly ship in which to sail. I was impressed by her smooth running, even at high speeds, and I was delighted that it was possible to keep exactly to our programme.'

On Thursday 11 May, with her docking programme completed, the *Canberra* left the dry dock and was manoeuvred alongside 106 berth for the first time. Two days later, on Saturday 13 May, she received a royal visit from HRH The Duke of Edinburgh who flew by helicopter from Windsor to make a private visit to the ship. That morning the *Canberra* was dressed overall and at just after 10.30am Prince Philip landed his helicopter at the heliport off West Quay Road. Waiting to greet him was Sir Donald Anderson and as he arrived alongside the ship many of the crew members lined up on the liner's open decks. Captain Wild welcomed his royal visitor on board and introduced him to the senior officers. He then made a tour of the ship during which he stopped to chat to a number of the crew. The highlights of the tour were the visits to the bridge, where the Duke signed the visitors' book, and to the engine room, where he took a keen interest in the control console which, of course, was the nerve centre for the machinery and electrical equipment. He was then shown the first class swimming pool, several of the public rooms in both classes and the galley. It was a fine sunny day and after leaving the docks at just after midday the Duke flew his helicopter out over Southampton Water and close in over the *Canberra*, which looked splendid in the summer sunshine.

Three days after the royal visit, on Tuesday 16 May, the *Canberra* was due to leave Southampton at midday to steam north for her acceptance trials in the Firth of Clyde. However, that morning a fault was discovered in a sea water cooling intake and her departure was delayed. Soon after this fire broke out in some of the engine room steam pipe lagging and, although the city's fire brigade was called out, the fire was extinguished by crew members who, because of the confined space, could only work two at a time. Finally, at 9pm that evening, some nine hours behind schedule, the *Canberra* left Southampton and set course down the Channel and up the Irish Sea for her official trials off the Isle of Arran. On board were 400 workmen,

Fresh from the builder's yard at Belfast the *Canberra* arrived in the Solent on the morning of 1 May 1961. Her funnels are still spotlessly clean in this photograph, but they would not remain so for long.

(FotoFlite)

On Saturday 13 May 1961, whilst she lay alongside 106 berth at Southampton Docks, the *Canberra* was dressed overall for a visit by HRH The Duke of Edinburgh who toured the ship. *(Southampton City Museums)*

foremen and technicians from Harland & Wolff's yard who were racing against time to put the finishing touches to the tourist class cabin accommodation.

The trials took place over two days and nights and during her speed trials on Thursday 18 May she reached a speed of 29·27 knots. The only real problems were caused by the widely used plate glass doors and screens which flattened the noses of a few unwary people, and some also got a wetting from the ornamental fountains in the tourist class lounge.

Canberra's trials were successfully completed on the morning of Friday 19 May and she anchored off Greenock where, at noon, at a small ceremony which took place on the first class section of the Sun Deck round the swimming pool, the vessel was taken over from Harland & Wolff Ltd by the P&O General Manager, Mr R. M. Thwaites and Captain Wild took command. Following this Harland & Wolff's trials master and his steaming crew left the ship and

were taken ashore by lighter, after which 600 passengers were embarked for a pre-maiden voyage cruise to Southampton. The passengers, leading shipping executives, journalists and travel agents, were the guests of P&O on what was to be a well-publicized coastal cruise from the Firth of Clyde to Southampton, whilst at the same time the workmen continued their efforts to complete the tourist class cabins. The *Canberra* left the Clyde at 10.30pm on Saturday 20 May and set course for Southampton. On this trip P&O were able to take full advantage of the fine weather and the holiday weekend to show off their magnificent new liner. By 7am the following morning she was off Douglas, Isle of Man, and by mid-morning she was close in to Holyhead. At 8.30pm she was steaming in the mouth of the Bristol Channel off the resort town of Minehead, and that night she continued her voyage along the north Devon and Cornish coasts, rounding Land's End at dawn on Monday 22 May.

The highlight of the voyage came at midday, when on a gloriously sunny day she entered Torbay. Whilst in these sheltered waters the ship stopped, thus enabling thousands of people to wave and cheer from the shore and hundreds of small craft were able to come in for a close-up view of the liner. On board the ship, at a small ceremony on the Sun Deck, Sir Donald Anderson presented the BEM to the *Canberra's* Chief Engine Room Serang, Sarfaraz Khan, who had been awarded the medal earlier in the year. After stopping once again off Exmouth the *Canberra's* stately progress continued until at 5.45pm she was off Ventnor, Isle of Wight but, instead of turning into the Solent, she continued her voyage along the south coast. At 7.45pm she was off the holiday resort of Brighton and just over three hours later, in a blaze of lights, she reached Dover. At 11pm she turned round and retraced her route along the coast and at 6.25am on Tuesday 23 May she secured alongside 106 berth in Southampton's Western Docks.

A splendid view of the Games Deck taken from the *Canberra's* terraced superstructure. The ship was on her trials off Arran at the time.

(Ulster Folk & Transport Museum)

With just ten days to go before she departed on her maiden voyage to Australia and the Pacific, the workmen continued with the fitting out, to which two extra tasks had been added. The first of these was to remove the fountains from the tourist class lounge, the William Fawcett Room. During the ship's trials these ornaments had proved to be impractical and they had continually spilled water onto the carpets and, in some cases, onto passengers who got too close. The second task was to remove the decorative ceiling in the tourist class smoking room, the Peacock Room.

During the stay in Southampton numerous parties of distinguished visitors were shown round the ship and entertained on board, including the government minister responsible for shipbuilding, Vice-Admiral J. Hughes-Hallett CB, who had commanded the aircraft carrier HMS *Illustrious* and who had been the Flag Officer Heavy Squadron prior to his retirement from the Royal Navy.

The *Canberra* had joined a passenger fleet of 17 liners with a combined tonnage of 418,000, but within three years the number of vessels would be reduced to ten and within 15 years only three would be left, one of them the *Canberra*. However, it seemed a good augury for the *Canberra's* future that on this occasion she was fully booked with some 2,238 passengers. A few of them were travelling only as far as Naples, but the great majority were sailing all the way to the Antipodes, among whom were 750 emigrants setting out for a new life in Australia, with another 120 going on to New Zealand. One family who must have got the best value from the *Canberra's* maiden voyage were the Parrett family from Ashford in Kent. There were ten of them - Mum, Dad and eight children aged three to 15 years of age - but all they had paid for the 23-day passage to Melbourne in the brand new ship was £20. As assisted emigrants Mr Edward Parrett and his wife both had to pay £10, but their children's fares cost them nothing at all. For them the voyage worked out at approximately two shillings a day for each member of the family.

However, for those who were paying their own way, single first class fares from Southampton to Sydney started at £275 per passenger, whilst the most expensive cabins cost £550. In the tourist class single tickets for the voyage to Sydney ranged between £180 and £235 per passenger, and for those who just wanted to be part of the *Canberra's* maiden voyage, a single tourist class ticket from Southampton to Gibraltar cost £16 and to Naples £26.

As well as this being the new liner's first commercial voyage, P&O were planning to do all they could to make it

The *Canberra* on her full-power trials in the Firth of Clyde. *(P&O)*

a goodwill trip and to show off the *Canberra* at all ports on the route, and it was estimated that when she returned to Southampton thousands of people would have inspected the ship. A series of cocktail parties and luncheons had been arranged on board for government and civic leaders, as well as shipowners, travel agents and journalists, with the chairman of the company, Sir Donald Anderson, travelling with the ship to act as host.

On the eve of the maiden voyage Captain Wild was appointed Commodore of the P&O fleet, while from Belfast came the news that Harland & Wolff had lost almost £2 million during the building of the ship. However, for the passengers who embarked during the late morning and early afternoon of Friday 2 June the excitement of departure day was paramount. The ship's sailing had been scheduled for 4pm, but due to a slight machinery defect it was 4.50pm before the last lines were released and five tugs of the Red Funnel and Alexander fleets pulled the *Canberra* out into the River Test. Hundreds of people were lining the balcony of the shed at 106 berth and balloons and streamers were released as the ship moved away from the berth.

All along the Weston shore, from the Seaweed Hut to Netley, vast crowds of people had gathered to watch the *Canberra* leave and cars were parked bumper to bumper on Southampton's east bank. As she passed Mayflower Park and Royal Pier the new liner was heralded by a raucous chorus of sirens and car horns and by the cheers of the thousands of well-wishers. One Southampton man who had not missed a maiden voyage in 30 years said that the *Canberra* was the most impressive vessel he had ever seen and that, 'I would gladly have missed all the others just to watch this ship.' As she passed the oil refineries at Fawley a thick cloud of black smoke belched from her funnels, and within two hours she was in the Channel and heading for Gibraltar. The *Canberra's* itinerary took her by way of P&O's traditional route to the east and two days after leaving Southampton she stopped off Gibraltar for less than an hour, which was just long enough for the mails to be transferred. At 7.20am on Tuesday 6 June she arrived at Naples and after a stay of ten and a half hours she left for Port Said.

During the morning of Thursday 8 June there was a moving experience when, six hours from Port Said, the

Canberra steams up-Channel to Southampton following her trials in the Firth of Clyde. This excellent aerial view shows her open decks to their best advantage, although her funnels are starting to become very dirty with soot. *(FotoFlite)*

Canberra passed the oldest ship in the P&O fleet, the *Strathaird*, which was westbound from Australia on the final leg of her last passenger voyage. The *Strathaird*, which was flying her paying-off pennant for the occasion, steamed close in to the *Canberra's* port side and the two ships' whistles blew in greeting. Captain Clay commanding the *Strathaird* signalled to Commodore Wild, 'You look magnificent and all in *Strathaird* wish you a happy and successful voyage and from the old to the new *Strathaird* bids you farewell.' Commodore Wild replied, 'You too look magnificent with your paying-off pennant flying gaily. You look a gracious and not too elderly lady. All well here.' As the two ships steamed past each other at a combined speed of 46 knots, Sir Donald Anderson made a broadcast to the passengers which literally moved some people to tears: 'It is perhaps a continuation of the P&O company's service that, as the *Strathaird* makes her last voyage home, she passes *Canberra*, the company's latest ship.'

The *Canberra* arrived at Port Said at just after 5pm the same day and, despite Commodore Wild's optimistic signal

to the *Strathaird*, it turned out that all was not well in the new liner. Trouble had developed in the port condenser and saline traces had been found in the distilled water samples, which indicated leaky tubes. Instead of joining a southbound convoy through the Suez Canal that evening, the *Canberra* had to wait while the ship's engineers carried out overnight repairs and it was 5.30am the following morning when she left Port Said to start her first transit of the canal. Following her departure from Port Suez later that day the ship's air-conditioning underwent its first real test as the *Canberra* steamed through the Red Sea for Aden. She arrived in the colony's inner harbour at 6.15am on Monday 12 June and originally she was scheduled to stay for 18 hours, departing at just after midnight on the following morning. Unfortunately, during her stay more problems arose with the condenser which culminated in a complete loss of electrical power and a very uncomfortable 14-hour delay in the port.

After leaving Aden at 2pm on 13 June she arrived in Colombo early on the morning of Saturday 17 June - over

12 hours behind schedule - and she left at 12.30am the following morning for the long passage to Fremantle where she had been due to arrive on 22 June. However, soon after leaving Colombo the condenser problems recurred and speed was reduced for the first time in the voyage. It was during the afternoon of Friday 23 June that she reached the Australian port for the first time, about 31 hours behind schedule. Despite this setback the *Canberra* received her first great welcome of the voyage with the Fremantle shore being lined with cars and cheering crowds. However, engine problems once again resulted in a delay and her programmed eight-hour stay was extended by an hour as the ship's engineers repaired a minor defect. Unfortunately, not long out of Fremantle there was a further recurrence of the fault in the port condenser and the great liner was forced to steam at reduced speed during her crossing of the Great Australian Bight en route for Melbourne where she arrived at 11.30am on Tuesday 27 June, well behind schedule. Despite this thousands of onlookers crowded the port quays and all the vantage points on the approaches, as well as the beaches of Port Phillip Bay, to watch the *Canberra's* arrival in Melbourne. One special guest who had travelled down from Canberra to see 'her' ship arrive and join her for the overnight passage from Melbourne to Sydney was Dame Pattie Menzies, her sponsor. Because of machinery problems which were being experienced the ship's stopover in Melbourne was cut short and after 24 hours she left for Sydney.

It was during the afternoon of Thursday 29 June 1961, over 24 hours behind schedule, that the *Canberra* arrived off Sydney Heads, where most of the port's small craft were waiting to welcome her. There were also several thousand people crowded on the foreshores to watch the great white liner, accompanied by the flotilla of boats, make her way up the harbour to berth alongside the Overseas Passenger Terminal at 3.30pm. At a press conference which was held soon after her arrival, Sir Donald Anderson announced that the faulty condenser which had caused all the delays had been repaired but, in order to be completely sure, the ship's engineers would be working on it during the four-day stay in Sydney. The arrival of the *Canberra* coincided with a visit by the Indonesian training barquentine *Dewarutji* and the local press were quick to appreciate the contrast between the old and the new.

The *Canberra* left Sydney on the evening of Monday 3 July and three days later she arrived in Auckland where, despite the thickest fog for 30 years which delayed berthing by more than four hours, a large crowd turned out to greet her. After a stay of just over nine hours the *Canberra* left New Zealand waters and steamed north for Hawaii and the port of Honolulu, where she arrived, after a five-day passage, on the morning of Wednesday 12 July. During the day many of the city's prominent citizens, including the State Governor, William Quinn, and the Mayor, Neal

Blaisdell, visited the ship together with Miss Hawaii, Miss Joan Vine, who presented the P&O chairman and the ship's senior officers with the traditional Polynesian garlands of flowers. The Mayor of Honolulu declared 12 July as '*Canberra* Day' and presented Commodore Wild with an illuminated manuscript.

After leaving Honolulu at 2am on the morning of Thursday 13 July, and in order to comply with US Customs regulations, the *Canberra* made a four-day passage to Vancouver where she arrived at just after midday on Monday 17 July. The day was clear with a beautiful blue sky and hundreds of small boats, including a firefloat with its gushing jets of water, turned out to greet the new liner. The welcome even included an impromptu fly-past by a score of light aircraft, and the tops of buildings were crammed with spectators all eager to have the best vantage point. It seemed that every shop window had a welcoming banner and there was a roaring trade in straw hats adorned with 'Welcome *Canberra*' ribbons. Both the P&O chairman and Commodore Wild were received at Vancouver's city hall and were taken on a high-speed drive through the streets of the city, accompanied by motorcycle outriders.

After a stay of almost 36 hours in the Canadian port the *Canberra* steamed south down the west coast of the USA, to arrive in San Francisco on Thursday 20 July. It was at 7am on that day, as the ship approached San Francisco, that Bellboy K. Copeland discovered a 26-year-old Australian man, Donald Harrison, hiding in a life jacket locker on the Promenade Deck. He had the dubious distinction of being the *Canberra's* first stowaway, having hidden aboard the ship two days earlier, hoping to remain undetected until he got back to Australia. However, after being escorted ashore in San Francisco, he was sent back to Vancouver. He may have been the first unwelcome visitor to the ship but would not be the last. As the liner approached the port she ran into a thick fog which did not lift until she had passed under the city's Golden Gate Bridge and entered San Francisco Bay. Fortunately, once the fog cleared it revealed a bright, sunny day and as the port's firefloats greeted the ship with plumes of water, a special welcoming ceremony was held. On Telegraph Hill, which dominates the harbour, a Union Flag was run up on the semaphore mast and two cannon thundered out a 13-gun salute, after which a US Army band struck up 'God Save the Queen'. Six riders on horseback galloped down the hill into the city centre to the Merchants Exchange carrying the word that the *Canberra* had arrived. It was a tradition with its origins in the days of the '49ers' when the sailing ships arrived after long and dangerous voyages across the Pacific, or from the east coast of the USA by way of Cape Horn. To commemorate this occasion the Californian Historical Society unveiled a plaque on Telegraph Hill.

As the *Canberra* made her stately way to Pier 32, which

It was an intrepid pilot who took this magnificent aerial view of the *Canberra* as she steamed towards Southampton from her trials on the Clyde, but it shows her cruiser stern and funnels to their best advantage. *(FotoFlite)*

Well-wishers, including one man who took to the roof of his Austin Westminster car to get a better view, wave farewell to friends and relatives as, at just after 5pm on Friday 2 June 1961, the *Canberra* heads downriver towards the Solent for her maiden voyage to Australia.

(Associated Press)

On the morning of Friday 9 June 1961 the *Canberra* joined a convoy to make her first southbound transit of the Suez Canal. She is seen here at Port Said shortly before her departure.

(P&O)

43025 "CANBERRA - 1961" Beken of Cowes ©

A splendid view of the *Canberra* as she manoeuvres the deep water channel in the Solent.

(Beken of Cowes)

The *Canberra's* maiden arrival alongside the Overseas Passenger Terminal, Sydney, at 3.30pm on Thursday 29 June 1961, almost 24 hours behind schedule. *(P&O)*

was packed with well-wishers, she was escorted by a fleet of small craft while overhead a squadron of helicopters performed a fly-past. Meanwhile, in the city itself 'Canberra Day' was celebrated with a parade which was said to be the biggest since President Eisenhower's visit some years earlier, and which was accompanied by a very noisy steam organ. On board the ship the terraced area round the first class swimming pool, which had been festooned with national flags and bunting, made a very attractive setting for the welcoming ceremonies which were televised and relayed to US and Canadian travel agents.

After two days in San Francisco the *Canberra* made an overnight passage down the coast to Los Angeles, where she arrived on the morning of Sunday 23 July to be greeted by a team of water-skiers, who had recently competed in the world water-skiing championships. The team were clad in swimming costumes bearing the 'Stars and Stripes', and were led by a young lady who had won the championship

and who skied alongside the *Canberra* performing impressive acrobatic moves. On the quayside the liner was welcomed by a platoon of US Marines and Miss Australia, who was in the city for an international beauty contest.

The *Canberra* left Los Angeles on the evening of Monday 24 July and retraced her route across the Pacific, calling at Honolulu for 24 hours on 28 and 29 July before setting course for New Zealand and the city of Wellington. However, what should have been a six-day voyage was marred by very severe weather during which the *Canberra* was unable to enter Wellington Harbour, and she had to steam off the coast in force 12 winds for two days before, at 3pm on 7 August, she was finally able to enter the port which had been closed to shipping during the storm. It was the first time that the *Canberra* had encountered such severe weather and Commodore Wild remarked that the ship had behaved 'like a lady' and there had been 'very little discomfort.'

From Wellington the *Canberra* returned to Sydney and

after only 24 hours in the port she set sail for Southampton by way of Melbourne, Fremantle, Colombo, Aden and Suez. She made her northbound transit of the Suez Canal on 28 August and then called at Naples three days later, on the last day of the month. On Friday 1 September, less than 24 hours after leaving Naples, the *Canberra*, steaming at 27 knots, overhauled and passed the beautiful Italian liner *Leonardo da Vinci*, which had been built as a replacement for the ill-fated *Andrea Doria*. After only a five-hour stop in

Gibraltar Bay the *Canberra* made the final leg of her maiden voyage in just under 48 hours, to arrive home alongside Southampton's Western Docks at 10.45am on Monday 4 September 1961. The voyage had lasted for three months and, despite her 'teething troubles', the passengers on this maiden trip had found her a happy and friendly ship, a sentiment which would be echoed by both crew members and passengers throughout the next 36 years.

A very impressive arrival at San Francisco on Thursday 20 July 1961, when fireboats turned out to greet the new liner.

(P&O)

Chapter Five

The New World And Back To Belfast

Following her return to Southampton *Canberra* remained at the port for 18 days during which a special 'Family Day' was arranged for her crew members. About 450 guests attended at Southampton Docks on Tuesday 19 September, some of them travelling from as far afield as the north of Scotland and Northern Ireland. Most of the relatives came down from Waterloo Station on a special 'P&O-Orient' express. During the visit the families dined in the Atlantic Restaurant and the ship's First Officer, Michael Bradford, made a short speech. Despite the fact that there was an electrical failure during the meal, which became a 'candlelight supper' the guests enjoyed their day on board as they were able to see for themselves the magnificent vessel on which their loved ones spent a great deal of their working lives.

Canberra was due to leave Southampton during the early afternoon of Friday 22 September 1961 for her second round voyage to Australia and San Francisco, but that morning a fire broke out in steam pipe lagging near the engine room control panel. Fortunately, it was not serious and was quickly extinguished by firemen who had to remove large piles of smouldering lagging and dump them on the quayside to be damped down. Finally, at 6.30pm, five hours later than her scheduled departure

time, the liner left Southampton. It was an unfortunate start to what was to be another troublesome voyage.

After a short stop at Gibraltar and eight hours at Naples the *Canberra* made her southbound transit of the Suez Canal on 29 September, calling at Aden three days later. It was during her crossing of the Arabian Sea, between Aden and Colombo, that problems arose when a minor stage blade in one of her main turbo-generators snapped, causing a reduction in speed from 27 to 22 knots. By the time the ship docked in Sydney, at 11pm on Wednesday 18 October 1961, she was a day and a half behind schedule and there were further delays at Honolulu while engineers carried out running repairs to the generator. Fortunately, the remainder of the voyage passed off without serious incident and after calling at San Francisco for 24 hours on 4 November she retraced her route, via Los Angeles and Auckland, to Sydney where she arrived on the evening of 21 November. Three days later she left for Southampton, once again steaming P&O's traditional route via Colombo and Suez, arriving back in her home port on the morning of Monday 18 December 1961 in plenty of time for Christmas.

The *Canberra's* third round voyage to Sydney and San Francisco started during the afternoon of Tuesday 2 January 1962 and once again she sailed by way of the

A fine view of the *Canberra* in Southampton Water as she leaves the port...

...on one of her early voyages to Australia.   (Ambrose Greenway)

Mediterranean and Colombo. Meanwhile, back in the P&O offices in London, discussions were under way with the intention of showing off the new liner on the North Atlantic in what was traditionally considered to be Cunard's territory. Although there were no plans for the *Canberra* to operate regularly on the North Atlantic, two cruises to New York were proposed as well as a short cruise to Madeira and Gibraltar and a longer one to Mediterranean ports. The company's 1962 cruise programme was to be the largest ever arranged by a shipping company, with 34,000 berths being offered in eight liners of the combined P&O-Orient Line fleet and 31 different ports of call being included in their itineraries. The *Canberra's* two cruises between Southampton and New York were the star attraction and with the minimum first class fare being £128 and a minimum tourist class fare of £72, it worked out at less than three pence a mile for the lowest priced tourist class ticket. These prices included all meals and accommodation and, of course, the ship was the passengers' hotel during their three-day stopover in New York. Nevertheless, the two holidays were marketed as complete cruises and not as line voyages, which would have necessitated P&O applying for membership of the North Atlantic Passenger Conference, which was not a requirement for occasional cruises.

However, prior to these events the *Canberra* was to make a fourth round voyage to Australia and the Pacific,

and once again the teething troubles in the liner's machinery were to receive a great deal of publicity. She arrived back in Southampton on Thursday 29 March and she was scheduled to depart again two weeks later on Friday 13 April 1962. However, the effects of the condenser trouble during her maiden voyage and the turbine problems of the second voyage were starting to show. The latter incident had meant that during her second voyage she had had to produce more power in order to keep up her scheduled speed, and this had resulted in the boilers becoming fouled up which called for a complete boiler clean. Her scheduled sailing was delayed for five days and then further delayed when, after embarking her passengers on Wednesday 18 April, problems arose with the main propulsion machinery. She finally sailed on the morning of 19 April 1962.

The continual problems with her machinery led to a decision being made to cut short her fourth voyage and return her to Southampton to undertake a one-month overhaul. The voyage to Australia was, as always, by way of Suez and she arrived in Sydney on Tuesday 15 May 1962 for a five-day stopover. From Sydney she steamed on to Auckland and into the Pacific, calling at Honolulu and then Los Angeles on Monday 4 June. Next day, instead of sailing for Vancouver and San Francisco, she steamed south for Balboa where she arrived on Sunday 10 June 1962. On the following day she undertook her first transit of the

With her hull streaked with rust after 96 days at sea the *Canberra* returns home to Southampton from the South Atlantic. *(Ambrose Greenway)*

With the skyline of Victoria in the background, the *Canberra* arrives at Hong Kong on a misty day in early 1988 on her world cruise. *(Ian Spashett)*

During June 1962, because of problems with soot staining, 5ft-high extensions were fitted to the funnels and soon afterwards the *Canberra* made her first cruise across the North Atlantic to New York. In this view, escorted by fireboats, tugs and small boats, she makes her maiden arrival in the port. She is seen here passing Ellis Island, with the Statue of Liberty in the background.

(Francis J. Duffy/South Street Seaport Museum, New York)

Panama Canal and, at that time, she was the widest commercial vessel ever to have passed through the canal. At one point the canal locks are 110 feet wide and, with *Canberra's* maximum width being 102ft - 5in, the clearance on either side was just under four feet. According to Commodore Wild: 'There was certainly very little room to spare, but we only touched the side once and then only very lightly.' At the time the *Canberra's* toll dues of £11,500 were the highest ever paid to the Panama Canal Authority. Fortunately, the passage was completed safely and after a short stop at Curacao, and another at Trinidad, she arrived back in Southampton on the morning of Thursday 21 June 1962 to be taken in hand by J. Thorneycroft for her first major refit.

Not only was the main propulsion machinery to be overhauled, but the opportunity was taken to make some necessary alterations to the ship's original design. One of the most important jobs was the fitting of 5ft-high extensions to the funnels in order to prevent the build-up of unsightly black soot marks down the back of the funnels. Initially the extensions were painted in traditional P&O buff funnel colour, but soon afterwards this was changed to black. Another major modification was the conversion of the first class Stadium area, just aft of the Crow's Nest. Originally, this space had been designed as a games deck which could be covered over during inclement weather by means of a sliding deckhead, but it had never

been a great success with passengers and so it was decided to create an area suitable for use as a theatre. This was achieved by welding the sliding deckhead into place and by constructing a large raised stage beneath it, at the forward end of the room just aft of the glass screens of the Crow's Nest. On completion of this work and the overhaul of the turbines, boilers and fresh water distillation plant, *Canberra* sailed on Friday 20 July 1962 on a seven-day cruise to Madeira and Gibraltar. It was the liner's first cruise and proof of its tremendous success was the fact that six first class and 14 tourist class passengers stayed on for the next cruise, the first of the special New York voyages.

The *Canberra* left Southampton at midday on Saturday 28 July with 1,800 passengers on board, all of whom were determined to enter into the party spirit and make a real success of the voyage. The North Atlantic is not, of course, noted for its 'sunshine' crossings, but the first day out was glorious and there was great excitement as the *Canberra* passed the *Queen Mary*, steaming eastbound for Southampton. Such was the occasion that the Sunday morning church service had to be delayed while passengers lined the rails as the two ships passed each other at a combined speed of over 60 knots. The rest of the outward voyage was overcast with patchy fog and so the ship's siren was regularly heard. As the *Canberra* neared New York the crew were busy decorating the ship with bunting and on her arrival at the Hudson River on 2 August, the traditional

The *Canberra* nears her berth in the Hudson River, New York. The sight of a P&O liner in New York was unusual in the early 1960s.   *(National Maritime Museum, London)*

When the *Canberra* arrived back in Southampton Docks on the morning of Saturday 11 August 1962, it was to a very full Western Docks. From top to bottom can be seen the *Orsova* at 101 berth, two Union Castle liners, the *Canberra* at 105 berth, the *Oriana* at 106 berth and the *Himalaya* at 107 berth. *(Southampton City Museums)*

Following the fire in her main switchboard during the early hours of 4 January 1963, the *Canberra* limped into Bighi Bay, Grand Harbour, Malta, at just before 10am on Saturday 5 January. Here she is being secured to a buoy with her lifeboats still out ready to be lowered to their embarkation positions. *(Associated Press)*

welcome was awaiting her. Firefloats were out as well as helicopters from the New York and New Jersey police forces, tugboats, and a mass of small boats. At 2pm she secured alongside Pier 91 where a band was playing, and the press were eagerly waiting to get on board to view the new P&O liner. The newly formed United States Travel Service displayed interest in response to President Kennedy's call for more tourists to visit the USA. For the *Canberra's* passengers there were four very busy days ahead of sightseeing and shopping, and the Broadway theatres to be enjoyed. On board the ship for the outward voyage was Paul Cunningham, a well-known NBC presenter who prepared a 'Canberra Special' which was transmitted over some 150 network stations. It was even said that President Kennedy himself watched the programme. Typical of *Canberra's* passengers was one lady who, as a secretary, earned just £10 a week, but she summed it up for many when she remarked, 'I never thought I would make it to America until I saw this trip advertised in a brochure.'

During the visit the *Daily Mirror* reporter, Brian Hitchen, was on board and the report he filed sums up the whole voyage: 'At first glance the inside of the *Canberra* looks less like a ship than anything I have ever seen. Magnificent inlaid staircases, murals of beaten metal which any Bond Street gallery would have been proud to own, and pastel shaded drapes were everywhere. This was not a ship, it was a huge floating hotel. I wondered whether I would ever find my way around her soundproofed corridors and ultra-modern spiral stairs. Two days and twelve hundred miles later I was just about familiar with the place. Three days at sea saw the last of the icy barriers

of traditional formality go down. Everyone was out to enjoy themselves.

Each morning brought an avalanche of gilt-edged invitation cards to cocktail parties all over the ship. And in the teenagers' room, the Pop Inn, *Canberra's* replica of a multi-coloured neon-lit London coffee house complete with jukebox, the youngsters were hell-bent on a glorious self-imposed task of twisting their way to New York. But it was *Canberra's* entry into New York Harbour that brought out the Sir Francis Drake in every man aboard. Never before, and I am not easily impressed, have I seen a more stirring sight. Down the Hudson River they came, the fleet of fussing tugs, fishing vesels, weekend sailors and just plain rubbernecks to gaze in awe at the towering majesty of *Canberra*, magnificent showpiece of British shipping. And having seen, they saluted in a cacophony of everything from the bark of klaxon horns to the deep-throated booming of ocean-going liners until the eardrums vibrated with the din and the mind boggled with the splendour of the reception.

All the way up the Hudson, through the welcoming curtain of spray thrown up by the fireboats of New York alongside the Statue of Liberty, the bunting-decked *Canberra*, her white Pacific bows knifing through the water, blew her siren in acknowledgement, returning the welcome of the New World. New York City Police helicopters circled her decks in a guard of honour, and when they peeled off, others took their place like worker bees round the queen.

It was two o'clock exactly when *Canberra* stood off New York's Pier 91 while her American pilot leaned on the bridge and, between those chews on a thick cigar, whispered instructions into a pocket-sized walkie-talkie and

A rare view of the ship's fire damaged switchboard, with light being provided by temporary leads and power being supplied from tenders which were moored alongside. (*Ulster Folk & Transport Museum*)

swung her into the quay with less effort than parking a car.

New York came - and four days and nights later - went in a haze of mammoth skyscrapers, cabarets, shopping sprees and swizzle-sticks. Sadly we were sailing down the Hudson in the sticky afternoon heat. The passengers were glum. But there was nothing that dinner and a new round of parties could not put right - and rapidly did. And so it went on. One 'fantabulous' string of mid-ocean race meetings, hilarious water sports in the three heated turquoise swimming pools, fancy dress parades and the stillness of noon when the navigation officer announced the ship's daily mileage total and the passengers chewed fingernails, wondering if they had hit the jackpot on the sweepstake.

And suddenly we were home. In the wheelhouse an officer obligingly pored over a complicated looking chart and told me: "We are exactly 75 miles from Land's End." I went below to my cabin and began to pack. We were home and the party was over.'

When the *Canberra* arrived back at Southampton's 105 berth on the morning of Saturday 11 August it was to a very full Western Docks, with the *Oriana* at 106 berth, the

Himalaya at 107 berth and the *Orsova* at 101 berth. Also alongside that day were two Union Castle liners, which gives some idea of the number of passenger liners which used the port in the early 1960s. Next day the *Canberra* left for her second trip to New York and on 27 August she sailed on a 13-day cruise which included the Mediterranean ports of Naples and Piraeus, arriving back at Southampton on Sunday 9 September to finish her first cruising season, which had been declared a resounding success.

It was on Wednesday 19 September 1962 that the *Canberra* sailed from Southampton for her fifth voyage to Australia and the Pacific, under Commodore Wild's command for the last time before his retirement. Most of the voyage passed without incident until the morning of Thursday 1 November, when she was leaving Vancouver for San Francisco in thick fog and she collided with a steel barge, *Van Bar 15*, which had to be beached. The *Canberra* stopped briefly for an inspection in case of damage, but apart from scratched paintwork all was well and she was soon under way once again. With all her machinery problems having been rectified during her refit earlier in the year, the *Canberra* returned to Southampton by way of Colombo and Suez and she arrived back alongside in her home port on the morning of Sunday 16 December 1962. It was the end of her first full year of service which, despite the earlier problems, had been a huge success. It was now the end of Commodore Wild's tenure as the *Canberra's* master and he was succeeded at noon on Friday 28 December 1962 by Captain Leslie Hill DSC who, like Commodore Wild, had trained at Pangbourne College and had served his apprenticeship with the New Zealand Shipping Company. During the Second World War, as an RNR officer, he had specialized in minesweeping and he had been awarded the DSC for his work in developing new techniques of dealing with mines. After the war he had rejoined P&O and his commands had included the troopship *Empire Fowey*, the *Iberia*, *Stratheden* and the *Chusan*. Two days after assuming command, at 7.35pm on Sunday 30 December 1962, Captain Hill took *Canberra* to sea for her sixth round voyage to Australia and the west coast of the USA. It was not going to be a pleasant introduction to his new ship.

At 8.30pm on New Year's Day 1963 the *Canberra* stopped in Gibraltar Bay for an hour and at noon on Thursday 3 January she put into Naples for four hours. After leaving the Italian port at 4pm the *Canberra* set course through the Tyrrhenian Sea and at midnight on the night of 3/4 January she passed through the Strait of Messina. Four hours later she was in a position Lat 37° - 18'N/Long 17° - 20'E, which was approximately 160 miles north-east of Malta in the Ionian Sea. She was steaming at 27 knots on a calm, clear night and she was due in Port Said on Saturday 5 January. By that time of the morning the passengers were asleep in their cabins and the only people who were up and about were the watchkeepers and nightworkers. This was the situation then, when, down in the engine room one of the officers on watch saw that one of the three turbo-generators had shed its load. He immediately tried to bring it back onto the switchboard using the standard procedure, but he was unable to do so and as the generator had not only come off load, but had started to 'motor', another member of staff also tried to get the machine back onto the board. However, he too was unsuccessful as he could not trip the circuit breaker and believing, mistakenly, that severe damage would result if the machine was left to motor any longer, he forcibly broke the contact in conditions which were not only contrary to recognized practice, but contrary also to a large warning notice which was posted on the spot. The result was an electrical arc of great severity causing a fire which continued to be fed electrically by the other two generators. The individual concerned had acted in good faith and taken the action which he thought was right, but afterwards the experts who examined the damage could not comprehend why the man had not been incinerated.

As the fire took hold of the main switchboard the immediate effect in the ship was the loss of all power and the sounding of the alarm bells. One passenger describes her experiences thus: 'I heard the alarm and immediately woke my husband and five children. There were no lights and it took me some time to find clothing for the children. The ship's crew were absolutely wonderful, but the smoke in the passenger spaces was rather unpleasant.' Another passenger remembers the thick black smoke: 'I had to fight through the smoke to get to the Promenade Deck and it was thick enough to make me cough, but everything was orderly.' Another passenger, who was travelling to Australia with his wife, recalls the choking black smoke in the vicinity of their cabin on D Deck: 'The smoke on D Deck was very thick and I could just see crew members dashing by. On C Deck we could breathe a little easier and the Promenade Deck was clear, but the only lights we had were from the lifeboats' floodlights.' Another passenger who was in the first class section had no problems with the smoke and he praised the 'resolution in the master's voice when he made the announcement. He asked us calmly to go to our boat stations and to take life jackets and plenty of warm clothing. Most of the ship was in darkness, but the emergency lighting soon came on and we found our way up top without panic.'

Meanwhile, down below in the engine room the engineers and the fire parties managed to bring the blaze under control and extinguish it within an hour. Fortunately, no one had been injured, but as a precautionary measure Captain Hill had all the lifeboats swung out to their embarkation positions and requested that the passengers muster at their emergency stations in the Promenade Deck public rooms. Once all the passengers were at their stations, Captain Hill was able to take stock of the situation. His great ship was lying helpless with no power on her main propulsion machinery, although essential services were being maintained by power from her emergency generators. In response to the crisis the *Stratheden*, which had left Port Said on 2 January for Naples, Marseilles and London, diverted from her course to go to the *Canberra's* assistance. Help was also at hand in the form of the Royal Navy and the cruiser *Lion* which, with the destroyer *Scorpion*, was exercising off Malta, as well as a rescue tug which prepared to put to sea from Grand Harbour. However, once the fire had been extinguished Captain Hill was able to put out a signal stating that he did not require help and that the ship's engineers were working to restart the engines. Even so the *Stratheden* continued to stand by the crippled *Canberra* and the RAF sent out a Shackleton of 38 Squadron, based at Luqa in Malta, to keep an eye on the situation.

At dawn the *Stratheden* was able to supply the *Canberra* with fresh bread and stores and during the morning the passengers were stood down from emergency stations. The Shackleton aircrew were able to report that many passengers could be seen relaxing on the Sun Deck or in the swimming pools in the fine weather. Later in the afternoon of Friday 4 January the engineers managed to restore power to the main engines and the *Canberra* was able to get under way at four knots for Grand Harbour, where the staff of Bailey's ship repair yard were preparing to receive her. During the night of 4/5 January speed was increased to ten knots and then to 14 knots as *Canberra*, escorted by the *Stratheden*, steamed through a Mediterranean swell towards Malta, where she arrived at just before 10am on Saturday 5 January. As tugs took control of the liner, the *Stratheden* continued her voyage but had to cut out her scheduled call at Naples and steam direct to Marseilles. By 11am that morning the *Canberra* had been manoeuvred into Grand Harbour and secured to a buoy in Bighi Bay where more permanent repairs could be carried out.

It had already become clear that the damage to the *Canberra's* main switchboard was so extensive that the voyage could not continue and that she would have to return to Harland & Wolff's Belfast shipyard for major repairs. However, P&O were faced with the immediate problem of how to convey the 2,230 passengers, many of whom were emigrants on assisted passages to Australia, to their destinations. To help resolve the situation P&O's deputy managing director, Mr F. I. Geddes, together with a team of engineering specialists flew out to Malta, while in London Sir Donald Anderson stressed that everything possible would be done to assist the passengers, although he had to point out that P&O would be unable to produce another vessel within a reasonable time in order to carry

On Monday 6 June 1994 the *Canberra* took part in the D-Day Review in the Solent to mark the 50th Anniversary of the Normandy landings. In this view, dressed overall, she lies at anchor at Spithead. *(Beken of Cowes)*

The day of the review was fine, but very windy, and to add to the atmosphere of the occasion hundreds of small craft also took part. *(The News, Portsmouth)*

the passengers forward. The only P&O liners which were in England at that time were the *Iberia* and the *Orcades*, and as they were both fully booked, to divert them would only produce further discomfort. He went on to say that the company had already started to organize a massive airlift, and that the first aircraft were due to arrive in Malta on Monday 7 January, with planes landing at Luqa Airport at four-hourly intervals depending on the airport's ability to handle them. It was also pointed out that any passengers who had paid first class fares for their voyage in the *Canberra* and who had to travel tourist class by air, would have the difference refunded by P&O. Likewise, if the air fare was more than had been paid for the sea passage, then P&O would make good the excess. It was also made clear that if any passengers wished to return to the UK then the company would refund the full passage money which had been paid.

Unfortunately, although 1,300 of *Canberra's* passengers signified their desire to continue by air as soon as possible, there was also a significant number who were refusing to do so. When press representatives asked Sir Donald about the so-called *Canberra* 'jinx' he answered, 'We have had more troubles than had been hoped for, any liner of such an advanced design as the *Canberra* was bound to have teething troubles.' He added, 'I still think the *Canberra* is the finest liner afloat.' Although he was absolutely right, one fact which could not be overlooked was that a fleet of aircraft was able to transport nearly 2,000 people to Australia within four days, and that did not bode well for the *Canberra's* future.

A number of the *Canberra's* passengers who were on the ship for the complete 'world voyage' left Malta on an Italian ferry for Naples, and from there they returned to Britain by rail. However, on the afternoon of Saturday 5 January hundreds of passengers met in one of the liner's public rooms to discuss the company's offer of alternative air travel to Australia. Mr Bob Marshal, a Sydney chemist who attended the meeting, said most people wanted to go to Australia by sea and, if not, they demanded that not only should P&O pay their fare back to the UK, but they should refund their passage money so that they could make other arrangements to get to Australia. On the Sunday an 'Action Committee' of passengers met in the Crow's Nest and 300 of them supported the motion to 'stay by the ship whatever happens'. According to one passenger who attended a meeting of the committee, the atmosphere was militant and he remarked that, had they been allowed to use the ship's loudspeaker, more passengers would have attended. He gave the author this account of the first meeting in the Crow's Nest. 'Mr Buckley, the chairman of the committee, said that the first of seven aircraft chartered by P&O would leave Malta that day at 1.30pm, and that 11 passengers had left that morning in the ferry *Citta di Tunisi*. He was frequently interrupted by some speakers who demanded instant action. "There are enough naval ships in this port to succour the British on board," said one. Another suggested, "Let's go ashore and find the British Government's representative and make this situation known to them." There were even demands to, "Find the Australian Government representative." Another voice from the crowd added, "And the New Zealand Government's too." Some passengers asked about the conditions under which they would be travelling by air, but there were shouts of, "We will not go by air - they cannot make us fly." One fiery Australian declared: "We will remain on this ship. I have my wife who is expecting a baby, and another 15-month-old child and my aged parents and I am not going to budge." There was a chorus of agreement when this same speaker concluded: "Let's stay here, all of us, and pass the ball into the company's hands." Some of the passengers expressed their own views that the company did not appreciate their predicament. One woman asked, "What happens when I arrive in Australia long before I am due, who will look after me, the company? Another Australian passenger remarked, "I'm staying here, even if they throw me into the Pacific."

The action committee members said they could not get satisfactory results and added that they were displeased with the way things were being run in the Bureau whilst the passengers were being interviewed to fill in a questionnaire yesterday afternoon. Without any air-conditioning the air in the Crow's Nest was hot, as was the atmosphere among those present.'

Despite all the hot air in the Crow's Nest, the reality of the situation was that the *Canberra* would be unable to support a large number of passengers, and Michael Cassar, a resident of Valletta, recalls the vast quantities of frozen food being unloaded from the *Canberra* and being landed ashore for burning because it had thawed in the ship's refrigerated spaces during the time power had been cut off. Meanwhile, the majority of the *Canberra's* passengers made the most of their unscheduled stop at Malta, and while many sunned themselves on deck, others found their way ashore where the Barrakka lifts operated a continuous shuttle service for the visitors. It was said that they even swelled the crowds attending the race meeting at Marsa. The Upper Barrakka area of Valletta bustled with activity as passengers made their way to and from the ship, and crowds of local people lined the railings to get a good view of the great white liner as she lay in the blue sunlit water off Bighi. Alongside *Canberra* was the naval lighter, *Ace*, which was supplying the liner with electrical power but, even so, large quantities of candles were being delivered to the ship since they were the only means of light for some cabins and for the Bureau. Two of the *Canberra's* launches plied continuously between the ship and the shore, but the demand was so great that the local dghajsas were also brought into service.

The P&O Company, meanwhile, were liaising with the Australian and New Zealand migration authorities on behalf of the assisted passage travellers and arrangements were made for their onward flights. Those passengers who were paying the full fare were asked to complete questionnaires containing the following options:

1) To continue to steamship ticket destination by charter aircraft.

2) To return to Britain by air.

3) To disembark in Malta for alternative arrangements and, if required, occupy hotel accommodation at the company's expense.

The final alternative was for the small number of passengers who were booked to destinations in the Pacific or on the West Coast of the USA and this was:

4) To fly to Australia or New Zealand, continuing by SS *Iberia* to the final destination. The *Iberia* was leaving London on 8 January 1963 and she was due to call at Sydney on 6 February, leaving for Suva, Honolulu, Vancouver, San Francisco and Los Angeles the next day.

Meanwhile Mr Buckley and his action committee, with the help of a local shipping agency, were hoping to charter a ship for at least 500 passengers. On Tuesday 8 January the Dutch liner *Willem Ruys* arrived in Malta on a world voyage and P&O were able to take up berths for 120 passengers who were physically unable to fly. *Willem Ruys* arrived in Malta at 8am and that morning there was a shuttle service between the two ships as the lucky passengers and their baggage were transferred from the *Canberra* in Bighi Bay to the Dutch liner which was moored on No 7 buoy near Crucifix Hill. The *Willem Ruys* sailed at noon that day and as she left Grand Harbour, passengers lined the decks on the starboard side to wave to the passengers lining the *Canberra's* rails, who cheered the Dutch ship as she departed. But this still left the majority who had to rely on British United Airlines at Gatwick who were organizing the fleet of large aircraft on behalf of P&O. This was no mean task, particularly in the winter of 1962/63 when severe weather conditions in Britain had already put other charter flights behind schedule. However, in the course of just a few days 14 Viscount aircraft were acquired and dispatched to Luqa in Malta to undertake the massive airlift to Australia and New Zealand. By Wednesday 9 January only 800 of the original 2,230 passengers were left on board, and half of these were flown on to Australia in Boeing 707s from Lufthansa. By this time there was a more settled feeling on board the *Canberra* as the remaining passengers resigned themselves to the fact that there was little alternative but to accept the offers which had been made by P&O.

This was a particularly arduous time for *Canberra's* crew as they not only had to assist in disembarking all the passengers' luggage, but there was also the heavy baggage, mail and even motor cars to be unloaded into lighters so that they could be transferred to the cargo ship *Woodarra*, which had put into Malta to take on its unexpected load. By noon on Monday 14 January 1963, with Bailey's ship repair yard having completed and successfully tested temporary repairs, the *Canberra* was ready to leave Malta and return to Belfast. It had actually proved possible to accommodate just 46 passengers, who were all genuinely unfit to travel by air, and by 1pm that day all other passengers had left the ship. They were all charged £24 for the passage, which was collected by an adjustment of the refund of their fares. At the time of sailing most of the tourist class accommodation was without any lights, and all the passengers occupying tourist class cabins were moved into the first class section. At the 'eleventh hour' it had been possible to fly a number of passengers to Naples where they embarked in the *Oriana*, and a final 50 left on a scheduled flight to Sydney.

At 2.15pm on Monday 14 January 1963 the *Canberra* was manoeuvred from her berth in Bighi Bay and 15 minutes later she slowly left Grand Harbour, sent on her way by waving, cheering crowds of local people who lined both the Upper and Lower Barrakkas to watch the departure. Shortly after leaving Malta she ran into 60-knot, Force 11 winds, and after a voyage of seven days the *Canberra* arrived at Belfast during the afternoon of Monday 21 January. However, due to high winds and poor visibility, she had to remain in Belfast Lough for over five hours before she was able to steam to her berth at Queen's Island where she docked at 8.40pm. It was 20 months since she had left the port for her trials and maiden voyage. Immediately upon her arrival the 46 passengers were disembarked and they left Belfast on ferries that same evening, bound for Liverpool and Heysham. The *Canberra* herself was taken over by Harland & Wolff in order that a new switchboard could be fitted and the fire damage be repaired. The opportunity was also taken to continue the general overhaul work which had been started in the summer of 1962 but which, despite the fact that she had to cut short her voyage by a month, had not been completed.

The repair work would take almost four months to complete and it was May 1963 before she returned to service.

The *Canberra* alongside Harland & Wolff's Belfast shipyard for major repairs to her main switchboard. *(Ernest H. Cole)*

On Monday 1 March 1965, whilst being towed astern from Sydney's Overseas Passenger Terminal into the harbour channel, the *Canberra* suddenly listed to port and the line to the stern tug *Woona* snapped. As the liner continued to move astern her mast struck the Harbour Bridge and was bent over at right angles. *(Ambrose Greenway)*

Five days after the *Canberra's* arrival in Southampton at midnight on Monday 16/Tuesday 17 May 1966, the National Union of Seamen called a strike of their members and many British passenger liners became strike-bound at various UK ports. In this view three Union Castle liners are alongside 101 berth, with the *Canberra* and *Arcadia* alongside 102 berth and the *Queen Elizabeth* being manoeuvred into 106 berth which had been vacated by the *Canberra*. *(Southampton City Museums)*

Chapter Six

The Last Liner Voyage

At 12.45pm on Saturday 11 May 1963 the *Canberra* left Belfast once again following the repairs to her badly damaged switchboard and the completion of general maintenance work in her boiler and engine rooms. For three days she underwent trials in the Irish Sea and English Channel before entering the Solent during Tuesday 14 May and anchoring for the night off the Isle of Wight. It was the following afternoon before the King George V graving dock became available and at just after 1pm she weighed anchor and steamed up Southampton Water to berth in the dry dock an hour later. Following routine maintenance on her underwater hull the *Canberra* was moved to her berth in the Western Docks, and at 2pm on Friday 24 May 1963 she left the port with a record 2,266 passengers to sail for Sydney where she arrived on Sunday 16 June. During the summer of that year a series of three cruises from Southampton had been planned, and in order not to disrupt these it had been decided that the first voyage following her repairs would terminate at Sydney and she would return to Southampton directly, by way of Colombo and Suez.

The first cruise of the 1963 season was a 14-day voyage into the Mediterranean, calling at Genoa and Piraeus, with the second voyage taking her to Istanbul and Piraeus. The final cruise was a 15-day voyage to New York and it was a repeat of the two successful cruises which she had made during 1962. She returned to the Australian route on Sunday 15 September when she left Southampton for Sydney, and following this she made three more voyages to Australia, returning directly to the UK and not steaming into the Pacific Ocean. Happily her mechanical problems had been resolved and the only incident which made the news happened on Friday 8 November 1963 when she arrived back in Southampton and struck the quay while docking. The incident occurred while she was being manoeuvred into her berth in a strong wind which swung her bows into the coping on the quay wall. Fortunately, the *Canberra* was not damaged, but about 15 feet of the quay coping was smashed.

On Friday 13 March 1964, during the return leg of a round voyage to Australia and only a few hours after leaving Port Said, the *Canberra* called at the Egyptian port of Alexandria. At that time she was the largest liner to call there and she was the first to use a new passenger terminal which had just been opened. *Canberra's* master recalls the visit: 'I was in and out of Alexandria during the war years many times, but I knew that it would be a very different port 20 years later when the *Canberra* came to make her

first call there. Considerable preparation was required for the reception of this, the largest ship ever to call, with her demands for depth of water and manoeuvring space, to say nothing of the needs of 1,600 or more passengers. The agents and port authorities had all done their best to help. A good lane through the shipping anchored in the harbour had been made and doubtless we were not very popular with the half-dozen or so ships kept plying in the offing while we entered. The new passenger terminal was quite luxurious and very elegant and has a vast marble hall with Egyptian decoration, all rather well done I thought. There was a team of uniformed girls led by the wife of a local doctor. She was the principal hostess, a job which she was doing as a hobby. She conducted the Staff Captain and myself all around the terminal to see the lounges, shops and offices, and in one VIP lounge we were given coffee and made to feel important by being introduced to senior officials as "His Excellency the Captain". Back on board we had a party in the Crow's Nest when the manager of the Maritime Shipping Agency presented the ship with a plaque to commemorate the visit. On the following morning I had a quick tour around the city and found it had not changed greatly since the war years, although we could visit royal palaces which, of course, were not open to the public in King Farouk's day. The harbour was full of shipping, Russian and Polish predominating, and we appeared to be the only British ship in the harbour and I was pleased that she was one we could be proud of.'

The *Canberra's* next foray into the Pacific in May 1964 became part of a round-the-world cruise since she returned to the UK by way of Acapulco, the Panama Canal, Nassau, Port Everglades and Le Havre, arriving back in Southampton on Monday 8 June 1964. At the end of the following week, on Friday 19 June, with 1,752 passengers embarked, the *Canberra* left Southampton once again for her first UK cruise of the season, a 14-day voyage to New York and back. It was the liner's fourth visit to the US port and this cruise had also been marketed on the Continent where a great deal of interest was being shown. The *Canberra's* visit to New York and her three-day stay coincided with the World's Fair which was being held in the city, and when the liner berthed alongside Pier 92 on Thursday 25 June there was a Dixieland jazz band to welcome her, as well as invitations to members of the crew to visit the replica of Captain Bligh's ship, *Bounty*, which was on show alongside the Fair. Once again the cruise was a resounding success and the *Canberra* returned to Southampton on Saturday 4 July 1964. Next day she

A very unusual close-up bow view of the *Canberra* and *Arcadia* alongside during the seamen's strike and...

...a stern view of the two ships together. (P&O)

sailed on her second cruise which took her into the Mediterranean to Naples and then on for her second visit to Alexandria, where she arrived on Sunday 12 July. The *Canberra's* last three cruises of the UK season took her into the Mediterranean again where her itineraries included ports in Greece, Turkey and Italy, with the final cruise ending on 3 September at Southampton. She then made a line voyage to Sydney which brought her back to Southampton on Tuesday 10 November 1964.

After fitting in one more round voyage to Australia which ended in January 1965, she left Southampton for the first voyage of the new year on Monday 1 February 1965. However, as she was leaving the Sydney Overseas Shipping Terminal at 3.15pm on Monday 1 March 1965, and was being towed astern from the terminal into the harbour channel, she suddenly listed to port and the line to the stern tug *Woona* snapped. As *Canberra* continued to move astern under the Harbour Bridge, her mast struck the bridge and the top ten feet of it were bent over at right angles. It turned out that the list to port had been casued by the vessel grazing a shoal off Dawes Point, and this in turn had caused the line to snap. Fortunately, very little damage was caused and the liner was able to continue her voyage to Southampton where she was docked for a more detailed inspection.

During the summer of 1965, between June and September, the *Canberra* made six cruises from Southampton, and when she resumed her line voyages on Wednesday 15 September she steamed into the Pacific by way of Fort Lauderdale, Nassau and the Panama Canal. Once into the Pacific Ocean the *Canberra* made two trans-Pacific voyages between San Francisco and Sydney which were marketed in Australia and the USA, and which proved to be very popular. By the mid-1960s P&O, like other shipping companies, were being forced more and more into holiday cruises, as the airlines with their bigger jet aircraft were making even greater inroads into the passenger lists of the large ocean liners. It was the start of a period of contraction for P&O, with the company having disposed of its entire pre-war passenger tonnage. However, there was to be no respite, and in the USA Boeing were pressing ahead with development of their 747 aircraft which would change the pattern of intercontinental passenger travel for good. During 1965 the P&O Company acquired the remaining minority shareholdings in the Orient Line, and so set in motion the final stages in the integration of the two fleets and the demise of the Orient Line as a separate company.

For P&O, cruising was the obvious answer to the competition from the jet airlines as the P&O and Orient passenger liners, with their extensive, wide open deck spaces, were ideally suited to this trade. In the mid-1960s it seemed that the future of cruising lay in the Pacific Ocean and in early 1966 the *Canberra* visited new ports as she

undertook cruises from San Francisco and Los Angeles. On Thursday 3 March that year she left the US West Coast to call at Honolulu and then went on to make her first visit to Japan. She arrived at Yokohama's South Pier on Tuesday 15 March and as she was manoeuvred to her berth astern of the company's *Cathay*, the Kanagawa Police Band struck up a series of welcoming marches. As soon as the gangway was in place, three young ladies all titled Miss Yokohama embarked to present Commodore J. L. Dunkley with bouquets of flowers while girls from a nearby High School lincd the quayside in their colourful, traditional kimonos, carrying 'Welcome *Canberra*' placards and waving sprigs of spring cherry blossom. Later, at a reception on board, the Commodore was host to local VIPs and, as is customary in Japan, gifts were exchanged.

A few days later the *Canberra* received a similar warm and friendly welcome when she made her first calls at Kobe then at Nagasaki. On Tuesday 22 March the *Canberra* made her maiden visit to the then British colony of Hong Kong and once again, not only was she the biggest liner to have entered the port, but her visit also opened the colony's new Ocean Terminal at Kowloon, which had cost 74 million Hong Kong dollars to build. It was this new terminal which enabled such big liners to call there and the most modern facilities were available for their passengers, including a shopping centre for those not inclined to venture further afield.

From Hong Kong the *Canberra* steamed direct to Sydney, before returning to San Francisco by way of New Zealand, Hawaii and Vancouver. On the last day of April 1966 she passed through the Panama Canal and after calling at Nassau, Port Everglades and Le Havre, she arrived at 106 berth in Southampton Docks early on the morning of Thursday 12 May 1966, straight into a major industrial dispute which would have far-reaching effects on all the major British shipping companies.

Five days after *Canberra's* arrival in Southampton, at midnight on Monday 16 May, the National Union of Seamen called a strike of their members and it was clear even at this stage that the dispute was going to be a long and costly one for both the Union and the shipowners. The *Canberra* had been due to sail on a short four-day Whitsun Cruise on Friday 20 May, but this was immediately cancelled and as notices were sent out to the unlucky passengers, the crew were paid off. Next came the question of a two-month long round-the-world voyage scheduled to begin on Tuesday 31 May, followed by two Mediterranean cruises during August.It was obvious that if the strike lasted any length of time this programme would be severely disrupted.

This was the first major industrial dispute by the seamen for 55 years and in the event it went on for 45 days. After such a long period of co-operation within the industry everyone concerned was asking the question: Why did it

A very familiar sight during the 1960s of the *Canberra* alongside Sydney's Overseas Passenger terminal, in the shadow of the Harbour Bridge.   *(P&O)*

and *Carmania*, which represented a bonanza for the small pleasure boats which offered harbour trips to view the splendid sight. On the other hand, however, it was a very sad and damaging dispute for the shipping industry.

When the strike ended at midnight on Friday 1 July, there was the enormous problem of getting the ships back to work in a way which would cause the least disruption to passengers. In the event it was decided to cancel the *Canberra's* two Mediterranean cruises and to dispatch her immediately on her world voyage, albeit over four weeks late. Letters were sent to all the passengers who had been booked on the cancelled cruises apologizing for the decision and explaining the reasons for it. Berths were offered to them on other cruises in August and September, with passage money being refunded to all those who could not transfer the dates of their holidays. Had the strike lasted another week, P&O would have been forced to abandon the world voyage and to keep the *Canberra* in Southampton for the cruises. Whatever the outcome of the strike, it left the management with a difficult situation in which inevitably a very large number of people would be disappointed. Faced with this problem it was felt that the world voyage must take priority since there were thousands of passengers all over the world, many of them away from their homes, all relying on the *Canberra* to get them to their destinations. Altogether the interruption of passenger ships' schedules had meant the cancellation of six cruises, including two by the *Arcadia* and one by the *Orcades* which was strike-bound at Tilbury.

The *Canberra* finally left Southampton for her world voyage at 1pm on Saturday 2 July 1966, sailing by way of Gibraltar, Piraeus, Port said, Aden and Colombo, arriving in Sydney on Thursday 28 July. She sailed five days later for Auckland and the Pacific, where she recorded another 'first' when she called at Nuku'alofa on the Tongan island of Tongatapu. It had been intended that *Canberra* would call at the island on 19 February that year, but this was cancelled following the recent death of Queen Salote Tupou and the fact that the country was in mourning. On

happen? It was quite apparent to the management that the main worry amongst seagoing staff was that a large number of NUS members wished to get to sea before the strike started and, equally, many of those who were at sea already continued to work loyally, even if they did express concern that their passage would end before the strike was over. The Southampton Port Authority had the problem of finding berths for all the large liners as they returned to the port and became strike-bound in the docks. By Wednesday 1 June the Western Docks at Southampton were almost full, with the *Edinburgh Castle* and the *Reina del Mar* doubled up at 101 berth, the *Good Hope Castle* at 102 berth, the *Vaal* at 104 berth and the *Canberra* at 106 berth. The *Arcadia* had to put into 47 berth in the Eastern Docks on her return from a 20-day cruise, and with more ships arriving every day, the port emergency committee took the decision to double up ships at most berths. On Monday 6 June the *Good Hope Castle* was moved to 101 berth, alongside the *Reina del Mar* and *Edinburgh Castle*, and on Saturday 18 June the *Canberra* was transferred to 102 berth where the *Arcadia* joined her after being brought from the Eastern Docks. The moves were all necessary to make room for the *Queen Elizabeth* which returned to the port that afternoon and was tied up alongside 105/106 berths. There was now a collection of 20 large liners including the two *Queens*, *Canberra*, *Caronia*, *Southern Cross*, *Oranje*, *Andes*

Canberra's arrival at the island her master, Captain E. G. H. Riddlesdell, who had taken over from Commodore J. L. Dunkley, went to the Royal Palace, accompanied by Staff Captain D. J. Scott-Masson and Purser E. W. H. Pinches, to deliver greetings from the P&O chairman, Sir Donald Anderson, to the new King, Taufa 'ahau Tupau IV, and present him with a Waterford crystal flower vase to mark the visit. That same day 34 Tongan VIPs were entertained to lunch in *Canberra's* Crow's Nest, while local schoolgirls gave displays of Polynesian dancing for the passengers who had gone ashore, making the short stay a memorable one.

On 29 August 1966 the *Canberra* made her eastbound transit of the Panama Canal and after calling at Nassau and Port Everglades she arrived in Southampton once again on Saturday 10 September. Seven days later she set out again for the Pacific, sailing via Panama and spending two months cruising from San Francisco and Sydney before finally returning home by way of Suez, five days before Christmas. On 23 December she sailed on a ten-day cruise to the Atlantic Islands and Lisbon, after which she sailed again for Australia and the Pacific in mid-January 1967. On 22/23 January 1967 she made what was to be her final transit of the Suez Canal for over eight years, because in June 1967 after the Israeli invasion of Egypt and their occupation of the Sinai, right up to the eastern bank of the canal, the waterway was closed to shipping.

The closure of the Suez Canal meant that the *Canberra's* next line voyage between Southampton and Sydney was by way of Las Palmas and Cape Town, and she made her first visit to the South African port on Saturday 17 June for a stopover of almost 24 hours. After leaving Cape Town she made the uninterrupted nine-day crossing of the Southern Ocean before arriving at Fremantle on Tuesday 27 June.

In the late 1960s another factor in the decline of the liner voyage between Britain and Australia was making itself apparent. In the 22 years between 1947 and 1969 some five million people, over half of them of British origin, had emigrated to Australia and of these 84 per cent had received assisted passages. It was these block bookings which did much to keep the tourist class sections on *Canberra* filled on her eastbound voyages from Southampton, but these bookings were declining rapidly and in 1970 there occurred two decisive events which would seal the fate of the liner voyage throughout the world. The first of these was on Friday 23 January 1970 when a giant airliner, the Pan American Airlines Boeing 747, *Clipper Constitution*, soon to become known as the 'Jumbo', flew across the Atlantic from New York to London. Despite widespread fears that such a large aircraft would disrupt airport schedules with the turbulence it caused, it landed safely and within half an hour the 362 passengers had cleared Customs and were on their way to their destinations. Six of these aircraft could transport more passengers to Australia within 48 hours than the *Canberra* could carry in three weeks. Once this high performance aircraft was flying regularly to Australia there was no hope that the *Canberra*, or any other liner, could survive as a viable economic unit on that route. The second factor to influence the liner's future involved the politics of the Middle East, where the long-term closure of the Suez Canal and the sharp increases in the price of oil would send many liners to a premature end in the shipbreakers' yards of Taiwan.

In October 1969 P&O announced that they would cease passenger services to India after February 1970, and during 1969 the *Canberra* spent most of the year in the Pacific Ocean, cruising from Vancouver and San Francisco. She made a number of 'firsts' by calling at new ports, most notably Miami, and Kingston, Jamaica. In the summer of 1970 she had a programme of four Mediterranean cruises from Southampton, but again most of the year was spent in the Pacific Ocean. Despite everyone's best efforts, many berths on the great liner remained unsold and it was clear that this could not continue. Less than ten years after she had entered service the *Canberra's* traditional role was redundant and in order to survive, a new function would have to be found for her.

Chapter Seven

Unsuitable For Worldwide Cruises

The 1970s brought no respite for the world's big passenger liners, or their owners, with the dual problem of more and more people travelling by air and the steep increases in the price of oil. However, in early 1971 the *Canberra* continued as usual with a line voyage to Sydney and when she left the port on Tuesday 16 February, her departure coincided with the disappearance of two young brothers, aged nine years and six years, from a city suburb when they were on their way home from school. Fortunately, two days later, the mystery was solved when they were found safe and sound on board the *Canberra* as she crossed the Tasman Sea, midway between Sydney and the New Zealand port of Auckland. They had apparently been trying to make their own way to Norway, their original country of origin.

Following her cruises in the Pacific, the *Canberra* returned to Southampton to carry out her programme of summer cruises, one of which took her to Santa Cruz, the capital of Tenerife. However, on 20 July, whilst leaving the port, the crew of the motor tug *Cepsa Segundo*, which was assisting the *Canberra*, were slow in casting off their lines and the tug was literally pulled under by the liner.

By early 1972, although P&O cruise bookings were up by 8 per cent on the previous year, many of the 47,468 berths on the company's UK cruises were not sold, and it was apparent that there would have to be a sharp reduction in P&O's passenger tonnage. The company commenced the cutback in April 1972 with the withdrawal from service of the 18-year-old liner *Iberia*. Later that month they announced that three more large passenger ships, *Chusan*, *Orcades* and *Oronsay*, were to be withdrawn within the space of the following 12 months, although, in the event, the *Oronsay* was given a reprieve which would keep her in service until 1975. During the summer of 1972 there were rumours that P&O was to join forces with the Cunard Steamship Company in the US passenger and cruise trade. It was even suggested that there was to be a merger between the two companies. It was said that the *Canberra* would enter the transatlantic market alongside the *QE2* with Cunard marketing the two ships for cruises on the east coast of the USA. According to Cunard's chairman, Victor Matthews, the talks between the two companies were: 'Only a straight honest endeavour to reduce our overheads in the States and help P&O with their marketing problems. Beyond that nothing is contemplated at the moment, but from a working relationship other things can develop.' However, P&O's spokesman was far more reticent about the future relationship between the

two companies, although it was admitted that during 1973 the *Canberra* would be based on New York for the first time, and that her programme of cruising would, '...follow broadly the same pattern of operation as the *QE2's* transatlantic summer service and winter Caribbean cruising.' It was also announced that P&O would be withdrawing from its regular line voyage schedules to Australia and the Far East, which would allow a maximum effort to be put into world cruising. During 1973 the company would only operate four round voyages to Australia and none at all to the Far East. It was clear that for at least two years P&O would be heavily engaged in the substantial streamlining of their operation, both the ships and the manpower. There would be some difficult times to be faced, and initiative would be required to find new roles for those liners which escaped the ever-hungry shipbreaking yards of Taiwan.

After arriving back in Southampton on Friday 5 May 1972, and after having undergone her annual 14-day refit by Vosper Thorneycroft, the *Canberra* began a series of five cruises from the port, all of which took her into the Mediterranean Sea and to the major ports of Spain, Italy, Greece and Turkey. However, with political tension between Israel and her Arab neighbours high, and with the Suez Canal closed to shipping, she cruised no further east than Istanbul, and she made her first ever visit to Trieste at the end of July that year.

During the late afternoon of Tuesday 22 August 1972 the *Canberra* left her berth in Southampton Docks for a round-the-world voyage which took her by way of Cherbourg, Port Everglades, Nassau, Panama and the West Coast of the USA. From Vancouver she steamed to Honolulu and Auckland and after leaving the New Zealand port on 27 September she suffered some damage to a forced draught fan and had to continue the voyage at reduced speed. After arriving in Sydney at 10.30am on Friday 29 September 1972, and having disembarked her passengers, preparations were quickly made to sail at 7pm that same evening for a three-day 'Cruise to Nowhere'. These three-day cruises, which usually encompassed a weekend, were very popular with Australian holidaymakers as they gave an opportunity for those with limited resources to experience cruising and to enjoy shipboard life. However, on this occasion the cruise was marred by acts of vandalism and hooliganism by groups of young passengers from the tourist class section. Drinking glasses were smashed in the bars and lounges, dozens of cigarette burns were left in lounge carpets which had been laid only

During the early 1970s, as the traditional liner voyages were replaced by air travel, the passenger liners turned more and more to cruising and this view shows three of P&O's liners, *Oriana, Canberra* and *Chusan,* alongside at Southampton and preparing for cruises. *(Southampton City Museums)*

a few months previously, and lifebuoys were thrown overboard. At one stage the troublesome passengers started to tear down cricket bats and caps from the Cricketers' Tavern, and an autographed test match bat together with an English county cap went missing. The ship's company, with commendable patience and tolerance, continually cleared up the debris and had to resort to removing as many items as possible from the Cricketers' Tavern, in order to save irreplaceable cricketing souvenirs. Senior officers patrolled the public rooms and decks in an effort to control the hooligans who, it was thought, were members of football clubs, but as soon as their backs were turned trouble flared once again and often it went on until the early hours. For the ship's company and for the vast majority of the passengers, there was some relief when the cruise ended on the morning of Tuesday 3 October, while the management were forced to give serious consideration to the discontinuance of such cruises. It was an example of how the disgraceful behaviour of just a few people can ruin a holiday for everyone. To their credit, the *Canberra's* ship's company had the vessel ready for sea again that same evening and she then made two cruises which took her to New Zealand and Japan, before she left Sydney on Tuesday 14 November 1972 and returned home to Southampton via Cape Town. She arrived alongside 106 berth in the early morning of Tuesday 12 December 1972, straight into an industrial dispute involving another of the company's ships.

The problems started on the *Orsova* on 13 December, when a large number of her Goan catering staff were dismissed following an outbreak of dysentry on board. The liner had returned to Southampton on Saturday 25 November 1972 from a West African cruise during which over 300 passengers and crew members had been taken ill, and as a result Southampton's Medical Officer of Health ordered tests to be carried out on all the catering staff. However, 212 of them, claiming to be victims of discrimination, refused and it was this that led to the dismissals. Feelings were running high amongst the Goan crew members and this unrest spread to the *Canberra* where 150 of the Asian crew walked off the ship to demonstrate solidarity with their colleagues who had been dismissed from the *Orsova*. Both ships were due to sail on 17 December for Christmas cruises, the *Orsova* to the Atlantic Islands and the *Canberra* to the West Indies, and P&O had to fly a senior member of the Indian Seamen's Union from Bombay to London, and then to Southampton where he was able to address the *Canberra's* crew. As a result of this meeting the *Canberra's* crew members returned to their duties and the ship sailed on time as did the *Orsova*, although on the latter ship only the first class accommodation was occupied and over 100 tourist class passengers were offered first class cabins at no extra cost, with the remaining 350 being offered an alternative cruise in the British India ship *Nevasa*, which

left Southampton on 20 December for a 14-day cruise. The ease with which these passengers could be found alternative cruises is an indication of just how many unsold berths there were on all the P&O Group liners still in service.

However, although the industrial dispute appeared to have been resolved, a new problem arose for P&O when many passengers on the Christmas Cruise became dissatisfied with changes to the ship's itinerary. Initially supplies of fresh water had been ordered at Curacao but, in the event, the required amounts were not available there and the ship's master was forced to divert from the scheduled itinerary to Port Everglades in Florida where he was able to restock with fresh water. However, this change meant that a call at Martinique, one of the highlights of the voyage, was cancelled and the ship herself was delayed by 24 hours. This led to protests from a number of passengers, all of whom were unable to spare the additional day as they had to return to their busy working schedules on time. As a result, P&O were forced to charter an aircraft and fly 91 passengers home from Madeira, the last port of call on the cruise. One of the passengers to leave the ship early was the former government minister Lord George Brown, who had important business commitments on the morning when the ship was due to arrive back in Southampton. Unfortunately, this concession by the company did not end the problem, and when the *Canberra* arrived at Southampton on Monday 8 January 1973, a further 120 passengers handed a petition of complaint to Captain Walter Vickers, the ship's master. One of the first class passengers who was interviewed by the press complained that, 'far from being a luxury cruise, there has been chaos from the beginning.' Despite the fact that the overwhelming majority of the 1,818 passengers were happy with the cruise, there was no doubt that the water shortages had been a problem and the company could not afford to ignore the complaints, particularly in view of the attention which the press paid to the liner's problems. To add to Captain Vickers' difficulties during the cruise, the ship's surgeon, Dr S. W. Watson, died at sea and the post mortem was carried out by a passenger who was a pathologist, as neither the Assistant Surgeon nor the Hospital Attendant could face carrying out the essential, but grisly, task on their former close colleague.

However, the New Year of 1973 brought the prospect of *Canberra's* series of cruises from New York and to prepare her for the US market she underwent a £100,000 refit to equip her for open-class cruising. The layout of the *Canberra* lent itself ideally to the conversion which proved extremely successful. Perhaps, from the passengers' viewpoint, one confusing area was in the vicinity of the cinema entrance on A Deck, which originally had been designed to allow access to both classes of passenger without one class encroaching upon the territory of the other. This in itself highlighted the anachronism of class divisions in the second half of the 20th century. On the

The *Canberra* in Southampton Water as she leaves on a cruise. In the background is the shoreline of Weston and to the right of the picture is part of Netley Abbey.

(FotoFlite)

The *Canberra* arrives in New York on Tuesday 30 January 1973, for what proved to be a disastrous series of cruises from the port. She is being escorted by the tug *Judy Moran*.
(Francis J. Duffy/ South Street Seaport Museum, New York)

Games Deck the former first class children's playroom on the starboard side became the Card Room, and the former tourist class shop at the after end of A Deck was replaced with the Gentlemen's Hairdresser. The Pop Inn, on the starboard side of the Promenade Deck, was converted into the photographer's shop, and an additional shopping area was provided next to the reading and writing rooms on the starboard side of the William Fawcett Room. The vessel's passenger capacity was reduced to 1,784, mainly by cutting down the number of four-berth cabins in the former tourist class section on A, B, C and D Decks. The *Canberra* was the first of the company's liners to drop the class barriers, but within 12 months all P&O passenger ships would be operating as open-class ships.

For her positioning voyage between Southampton and New York, 250 berths were sold at the cheapest price of £39 and 350 at £49, while the return package, which included the air fare to London, started at £69. When she left Southampton on Wednesday 24 January 1973, *Canberra* became a dollar-based ship and, to cater for the US market, a casino was opened on board - the first on any P&O ship. She arrived in New York, after a very rough passage, on Tuesday 30 January 1973 to start the company's programme of 19 cruises which ranged from seven to 15 days duration. During her hectic 36-hour turnround in New York, three major receptions were held on board for civic dignitaries, representatives of the press and the travel trade. During these events Captain Eric Snowden, the *Canberra's* master, made sure that the liner and her cruise programme received the maximum amount of publicity. Unfortunately, despite his efforts, advance bookings were disappointing and it highlighted the fact that, although P&O's liners were popular on the West Coast of the USA, they were not so well known on the East Coast.

Canberra left New York on Wednesday 31 January 1973 for her first ten-day cruise to the West Indies, which took her to Grenada, Barbados and St Thomas, while her second cruise, which was for 14 days, took her to Nassau, Port au Prince, Haiti, La Guaira, the port for Caracas in Venezuela, Barbados, Fort de France, Martinique, and St Thomas. However, despite these exciting itineraries, the bookings for *Canberra's* cruise programme remained depressingly low and when she returned to New York on Saturday 24 February it was announced that the next cruise was cancelled. During the following day, while shore staff feverishly endeavoured to find her a lay-up berth, the *Canberra* lay alongside until finally, at 8.30am on Monday 26 February, with only essential crew members on board, she left New York for Wilmington, North Carolina. At 6.30pm the following day the *Canberra* arrived at her anchorage at the mouth of the Cape Fear River, six miles from the nearest land and 30 miles from the city of Wilmington itself, which was really too far away for the majority of the city's residents to be aware of the presence of the unusual visitor. The nearest outpost for the officers and crew members who remained on board the *Canberra* was the small fishing village of Southport, which was an hour's journey away by launch. At that time of the year, with many of the fishing boats laid up and the motels closed, it was a quiet, sleepy, little place with a small shopping complex and tree-lined residential streets. Down at the boat harbour was Louis' Fine Foods, a local café where many of the *Canberra's* complement were introduced to 'grits' with eggs and 'hush puppies', steak and sweet potato pie.

The *Canberra's* main link with the shore was maintained by a fishing launch which was owned and operated by a local man, Dick Skipper, or, as he became known to the liner's crew, 'Skipper Dick'. He brought out mail and newspapers from the shore and took away bags of garbage. However, this link was rather tenuous, for when a storm from the Atlantic blew up or when thick fog covered the area, he was unable to get out to the ship. When he could reach the liner the transfer from ship to launch was quite hazardous as it required a flying leap from the galley gun-port door on E Deck to the fore deck of the launch. Getting back on board the liner was even more difficult and it needed a keen eye to judge the correct moment to make the leap. After an initial surge of interest in their surroundings, the limitations of the village of Southport and the expense of getting into Wilmington by taxi discouraged most of the crew from going ashore and they resigned themselves to staying on board. It was not long before the Staff Captain, J. A. Lefevre, and the Welfare Leading Hand had organized a varied programme of entertainment with films and TV shows from local stations, as well as bingo sessions and a four-a-side football competition, which was won by one of the Goan teams. Perhaps the highlight of the football matches was a 'special' between the five ladies who had remained on board, and the senior officers. The ladies won by six goals to four and, to the huge delight of the spectators, the Staff Captain was sent off for 'handling the lady' instead of playing the ball.

However, despite these light-hearted interludes there was a recognition by those on board that the future of the *Canberra* was uncertain and it was with some relief that the liner's crew weighed anchor at 6.20pm on Tuesday 20 March 1973, to return to New York to complete the final nine cruises of the scheduled programme. It was 8.50am on Friday 23 March when the *Canberra* arrived alongside her berth in the Hudson River. With winter over the bookings for her cruises, whilst still well short of full capacity, were improving and on Saturday 24 March the *Canberra* left for the West Indies.

Back in London the company's management struggled to come to terms with the realities of the changes which had taken place within the passenger division of the shipping company, and on Friday 1 June 1973, as the *Canberra* was nearing the end of a 14-day cruise to the Caribbean, a press conference was held at P&O's head office in London. Mr Richard Adams, the P&O Group executive director with overall responsibility for the passenger division, announced that on completion of her New York cruise programme, at the end of September that year, the *Canberra* was to be withdrawn from service. He went on to tell the conference that between January and September the operational loss on the ship would amount to £500,000. He commented, 'Unlike our other passenger ships, in both economic and operational terms, *Canberra* has proved unsuitable for the worldwide cruising role she has had to assume.' The news came like a bombshell to the shipping world and Mr Adams had little comfort for his audience when he went on to say: 'A feasibility study is at present being carried out to ascertain whether it is technically possible to re-engine the ship to reduce her operating draught from 35$\frac{1}{2}$ft to about 32ft. Should the exercise prove impracticable or too costly *Canberra* will be sold. In financial terms, if the re-engining exceeds £3,000,000 the ship will be sold.' The fact was that *Canberra's* biggest drawback was her 35$\frac{1}{2}$ft draught, which meant that there were a limited number of ports she could use during her cruises. On the question of a buyer for further trading, Mr Adams said that P&O would require, 'a

substantial premium over scrap value from any purchaser to prevent a conflict of interests.' He horrified many of those in the audience by speculating that one company who might be interested in the ship was the C. Y. Tung Group who, following the loss of their *Seawise University* (ex-*Queen Elizabeth*), might consider the *Canberra* for use as a floating university.

More gloomy news followed when Mr Adams announced that there were likely to be over 500 redundancies, the majority of which would be amongst sea-going staff. He ended by reporting that *Canberra* had been losing money for the past two years and that the New York cruise season had proved to be a disaster, with the best booked cruises being only 30 per cent full.

The news was a terrible shock to P&O employees and particularly to the *Canberra's* crew members, whose mood is summed up by Roger Chapman, a radio officer who was serving with P&O at that time: 'P&O's decision to withdraw the *Canberra* in 1973 caused much gloom and despondency, both in her and in the *Oriana*, with their large crews. This was a time of generally low morale, with shifting trade patterns, reduced manning and a boardroom battle which resulted in the rise to power of Lord Inchcape. The plans for the withdrawal of the *Canberra* were so far advanced that new radio equipment for her was diverted to the *Oriana*, where all the pre-assembled cabling was found to be unsuitable.'

Meanwhile, back in the USA, the *Canberra* continued with her Caribbean cruise programme, oblivious to the wry 'I told you so' comments from those naval architects and engineers who had decried John West's designs back in the late 1950s. One particularly interesting cruise which took place during the summer of 1973 was a 15-day voyage across the Atlantic with calls at Tenerife and Dakar which had been organized by an academic who had successfully arranged a cruise in the Greek liner *Olympia* to witness a partial eclipse of the sun off the east coast of Canada. This time he intended that the *Canberra's* passengers should witness a total eclipse which would be the second longest in recorded history and which would not be bettered until the year 2150. It turned out that the *Canberra*, with her spacious and open Sun Deck, was the ideal ship for the astronomers and after having been advertised in scientific magazines, the 'Eclipse Cruise' was fully booked. The story can be taken up by Alan Hale, the *Canberra's* Purser: 'During the brief layover in New York (20 June to 23 June) before sailing on the cruise, the incredulous but curious eyes of the crew witnessed the loading of large amounts of strange and bizarre equipment and the transformation of the public rooms from their usual role of being entertainment areas to that of lecture halls and instruction centres. Perhaps the greatest single change of all was in the Meridian Room where the blackjack tables and roulette wheel of the casino gave way to "Serendipity Hall", a specially designed exhibition of scientific projects and information loaned by various organizations, including NASA.

The entertainment staff stood back amazed that our passengers were not interested in discos, dances, casinos, bingo and one might almost add, alcohol. A typical day's activities were so different from our usual programme, the day starting with the bird watchers getting together on A Deck aft at 6.30am, continuing with only brief pauses, with lectures on meteorology, astronomy, oceanography, the history of science, the Apollo project, photography, navigation and so on, ending up at 11pm with celestial observations on the upper deck. The staff presenting this wide-ranging series of talks included many well known names, among them were Professor Neil Armstrong, the first man to set foot on the moon in July 1969, Mr Scott Carpenter, an aquanaut as well as an astronaut, and Doctor Isaac Asimov, a man of many talents.

And so to the anxious glances at the sky that Saturday morning, 30 June 1973. In spite of moving from our planned position during the night, in the hope of finding better conditions, the day dawned overcast and hazy. Sandstorms over the Sahara were said to be responsible. By 9am, 16 minutes before the first contact, the cloud had begun to clear and it soon became evident the situation would be saved and the viewing of the solar eclipse would be a success.

From the moon's shadow first touching the sun to its clearing it again was over two and a half hours, but the actual period of totality was five minutes 45 seconds. By moving in search of clear skies we had unfortunately forfeited a precious minute of the totality. The ship was 300 miles off the coast of Mauretania. All the possible machinery was shut down, lights were turned off and we drifted in a calm sea, while our scientists, professional and amateur, pointed their battery of cameras, telescopes and other more sophisticated instruments at the dying sun. The open decks were an incredible sight, a virtual forest of tripods and mounted equipment. As totality approached it began to grow dark and there was a noticeable drop in temperature. All colour was drained from the sea and sky. When first the diamond ring and then Bailey's Beads had gone and the last rays of sunlight disappeared behind the moon, there was a spontaneous round of applause, accompanied by a mixture of "oohs" and "aahs" from the assembled passengers. We saw the corona, composed of gaseous flares from the sun, stretching into the blackness around the moon and Sirius, Pollux and other first magnitude stars were visible in the sky. To me the supreme moment was when the sun suddenly shone out again like a beacon, as it showed above the rim of the moon in the second diamond ring, and light flooded back into the world. It was pure magic. All of us present in *Canberra* at that time were privileged to have seen an unforgettable sight.'

The *Canberra* arrived back in New York on the morning of Sunday 8 July 1973, and she sailed again that evening,

this time for a ten-day cruise to the Caribbean. Her first port of call was at St George's, the capital of the West Indian island of Grenada, where she arrived during the morning of Thursday 12 July. At 8.50am, whilst she was manoeuvring to anchor, she ran aground on Lloyd Shoal to the south of the harbour. The forward two-thirds of her length were stuck fast on a seabed of sand and dead coral, and although the ship's engines were manoeuvred in an attempt to refloat her, this proved unsuccessful and so they were stopped. Fortunately, weather conditions were good and it was soon ascertained that there was no damage to the ship, and therefore neither the passengers nor the vessel were in any immediate danger. Assistance was requested in the form of tugs, and barges for lightening the ship, and while they were awaiting their arrival, the crew made further attempts to refloat her. However, despite trimming and ballasting, *Canberra* remained stuck fast, and at 11.40pm that evening the Venezuelan tug *El Buey Grande* arrived on the scene and Captain Lefevre held discussions with the tug master as to the best way of refloating his ship.

At 1.10am on Friday 13 July a second Venezuelan tug, the *R. W. Cardon*, arrived and she was made fast to the *Canberra's* starboard quarter, with the *El Buey Grande* being secured to the liner's port quarter. At 2.53am the tugs started towing astern and seven minutes later the *Canberra's* engines were manoeuvred astern to aid the ship in clearing the shoal. Despite these efforts being maintained for over three hours, the liner remained grounded and at 6.20am the manoeuvres were suspended. Further attempts to refloat the *Canberra* were tried at 11am that morning, again without any success, and the next effort started at 1pm that afternoon, with the two tugs pulling and the *Canberra's* main engines being manoeuvred at 'full astern'. Once again the attempts failed and at 2.30pm there was a tragic end to the effort when a tow line to the tug *R. W. Cardon* snapped. The end of the broken tow rope recoiled through an open port in the laundry on the starboard side of E Deck and struck Laundryman Rozario Gomes in the face. The unfortunate individual received severe crush injuries to his face and the ship's Assistant Surgeon, Mr T. T. Spare, certified death as having been instantaneous. This terrible accident ended that particular attempt to refloat the liner and it was four hours later, at 6.30pm, that the next attempt was made, once again without any success.

On the morning of Saturday 14 July 1973, with *Canberra* still refusing to move from Lloyd Shoal outside St George's Harbour, the Purser's department began to make preparations to fly home the ship's 1,600 passengers. Arrangements were made for the charter of a number of short-range jet aircraft to airlift the passengers from Grenada to St Lucia, from where they would be flown home to New York. However, as these arrangements would take some time to complete, efforts continued in the meantime to refloat the liner. The final attempt involving

The *Canberra* steams north through the Suez Canal during a world cruise.

(E. A. Azab, Suez Canal Authority)

The old and the new. The brand new *Oriana* is manoeuvred past the *Canberra* at Southampton on 8 April 1995.

(M. Beckett)

the two tugs was made at 5.55pm on Saturday 14 July, and two hours later, with still no success, the *El Buey Grande* was dismissed. At 11.50pm that night another tug, the *Elena H*, arrived with an empty fuel barge in tow and at 2.50am on Sunday 15 July the *Canberra* commenced transferring bunkers to the barge. The fuel transfer lasted for just over four and a half hours and at 7.25am, with 500 tons having been removed, it was decided to make a further attempt at refloating the stranded liner. This got under way at 7.32am, and two minutes later the *Canberra* cleared the shoal and was immediately manoeuvred to her anchorage, nearly three days later than originally scheduled. The ship's carpenter soon reported that all soundings were correct, and a diver was employed to inspect the underwater hull. He reported that the only damage to the vessel was a small amount of scored paintwork which started about 100ft from the forefoot and reached 20ft aft on the starboard side of the keel plate, some 10ft from the centre line. The passengers then had the opportunity of a day ashore while the 500 tons of bunkers were pumped back on board from the lighter, and at just after 8pm that evening the *Canberra* weighed anchor to continue the cruise.

As a result of the delays at Grenada, the liner's proposed call at Martinique was cancelled and she proceeded to Barbados and St Thomas on 16 and 17 July respectively, returning to New York three days later. She berthed there at 9.30am on Friday 20 July, at the end of a very eventful two weeks and what should have been a routine cruise.

The *Canberra's* next cruise, a seven-day voyage to the West Indian islands of St Thomas and St Martin, started the next day and this was followed by a two-week Caribbean cruise which ended on Saturday 11 August back in New York. She sailed again that evening at 7pm, and on the morning of Tuesday 14 August she arrived at St Thomas, the US island in the Greater Antilles. She anchored off the harbour of Charlotte Amalie at 11.10am without any problems, but early in the evening a severe squall with abnormally high winds blew up, and at 7.30pm the *Canberra* dragged her anchor and went aground in about 30ft of water at the entrance to the port. Once again the engines were manoeuvred in an attempt to refloat the ship, but as in the previous incident this was to no avail. Later that evening two of the ship's launches got into difficulty while returning from the shore, but they eventually made it back safely, and at no time were the liner's 1,800 passengers in any danger on board. The *Canberra* was aground on sand and soft coral with 60 per cent of her port underwater hull, including her port stabilizer and port rudder, embedded there. She was situated due east of Sprat Point, south-east of Water Island, with her bow pointing north, hooking the 30ft curve, with about 19ft of water at her lee shore. She had a 2° list to port and as she was buffeted by the strong beam winds the ship's log described her as, 'lively'. It stated her position as

'Lat 18° - 19'N/Long 64° - 56'W, with deep water from 10° on the port bow, all around the starboard side and to 45° on the port quarter.'

The same evening P&O instructed their agents in Charlotte Amalie to engage the salvage tugs *R. W. Cardon* and the *Don Marie*, which were thought to be 48 hours away from St Thomas at that time, and it looked as though everyone was preparing for another difficult task. Fortunately, the *R. W. Cardon* and another tug, the *Elena H* arrived on the scene the next day, bringing with them an empty fuel barge into which 400 tons of bunkers could be transferred. This time all the efforts of the ship's engineers and the two tugs paid off, and later that evening the liner was refloated and anchored safely in the deep water channel. Next day divers were sent down to inspect the ship's underwater hull and they were able to report that although there was some scraping there were no indentations. Although they found that the tips of the starboard propeller were bent, there was no really serious damage and approval was given for the repair work to await the ship's next dry docking.

Following the survey, and after having taken back on the bunkers which had been discharged, the *Canberra* left Charlotte Amalie at 6.40pm on Thursday 16 August and after calling at St Martin the next day, she arrived back in New York at 10am on Monday 20 August. Once again the liner's deep draught had proved to be a serious problem, showing that she was clearly limited to deep water ports. It seemed that the ship's critics had been proved absolutely correct.

However, back in London during the evening of Tuesday 14 August, whilst the *Canberra* was aground and helpless, a press conference was called at P&O's head office in Leadenhall Street, London. There, to the surprise of all those present, it was announced that the *Canberra* was not to be withdrawn from service after all. The reason given for this volte-face was a sudden demand for last minute cruise bookings, which were running at double the rate that P&O would normally expect at that time of the year. Other shipping companies reported a similar trend which was attributed largely to people switching from European holidays to cruises because of international currency fluctuations. However, there were also strong rumours of a boardroom battle within the company but, whatever the reasons, the *Canberra* could look forward to a whole new career as a cruise ship.

In the short term, however, following the completion of her ill-fated cruise programme, she left New York on 28 September 1973 to return to Southampton via Cherbourg. She arrived in her home port on the morning of Friday 5 October to undergo a ten-week refit during which further work would be carried out to improve her open-class cruising facilities.

Although it was difficult to see it at the time, the *Canberra's* future was now assured.

Chapter Eight

Canberra Cruises The World

Following the Suez debacle of 1956 Britain's retreat from Empire was both swift and irreversible, and by the mid-1970s the new gods for the British public were economic growth and consumer spending. For P&O, whose origins lay in Empire trade, new opportunities were presenting themselves, for with greater consumer spending there came a dramatic growth in the leisure industry and particularly in the demand for foreign holidays. The P&O liners were ideally suited for cruising in hot climates with their spacious open decks and open-air swimming pools, and in addition their white livery lent itself to easy marketing of sunshine holidays. However, the UK cruising season was clearly only viable between March and November and there remained the problem of how to employ the ships profitably during the winter months. The answer, of course, was to send the vessels on a round-the-world voyage, which the *Canberra* and other P&O liners

An interesting stern view of the *Canberra* in dry dock at Southampton as maintenance work is carried out on her propellers and A brackets. *(Vosper Thorneycroft Ltd)*

had already been doing for nearly ten years. The continued closure of the Suez Canal was inconvenient and meant that ships had to be routed by way of Cape Town, but with a growing demand for such cruises, which were marketed as an all-in package or in sections as fly-cruises, this was not seen as a major problem.

With four of its large passenger ships having been withdrawn from service during 1973 and with the growing demand for open-class cruises, P&O's five remaining liners were now easily filled. Indeed, such was the increase in demand that had berths been available, 5,000 more passengers could have been accommodated for the 1974 cruise programme. By keeping the *Canberra* in service and by transferring her to the UK, the number of available berths was increased substantially.

When the *Canberra's* refit ended on 15 December 1973, she left Southampton that same evening for a three-week Christmas and New Year cruise to the Caribbean which had originally been planned for the *Orsova* before she was withdrawn from service a month earlier, on 15 November. By scrapping the older ex-Orient Line vessel instead of the *Canberra*, P&O had avoided a costly conversion of the *Orsova* from her two class configuration to open class. It was announced that the *Canberra* would, in future, operate from Southampton between April and December each year, with an annual world cruise between January and April. In 1974 she undertook what would have been *Orsova's* world cruise and then she went on to implement that liner's 1974 cruise programme. Passengers who were already booked on the ex-Orient Line ship were transferred, at no extra cost, to the *Canberra* and in many cases enjoyed superior accommodation. It was intended that the *Canberra* would operate in conjunction with the 42,000-ton *Oriana*, with the two ships calling at different ports for which they were particularly suited.

With the advent of full-time cruising the needs of passengers were now very different from those of the emigrants seeking to start a new life in Australia. Within the space of the average two-week cruise the holidaymakers wanted to enjoy all the activities which had previously taken place during a leisurely four-week voyage to Australia. In addition they also wanted more sophisticated entertainment programmes such as those which had been part of the US cruising scene for some years. Prior to 1973 all the passenger entertainment had come under the direction of a ship's Staff Captain, assisted by liaison officers and hostesses in both first and tourist classes. The Staff Captain had usually presided over a committee of

A close-up view of the *Canberra's* starboard A bracket, propeller and her rudder. The men carrying out the maintenance work put the size of the ship into perspective. *(Vosper Thorneycroft Ltd)*

turn them into hostesses in 24 hours, but I could not turn a hostess into a dancer. This became the policy so that quality West End revues could be put on, and potted versions of all the musicals were performed.' Staff working in the entertainments department were subjected to a very demanding routine with an 18-hour day being quite normal, rehearsals being fitted in during port stopovers when most passengers were ashore.

However, for some diehard passengers who had stuck loyally to P&O since pre-war years, the new cruises being offered were difficult to come to terms with. This point is exemplified by one wealthy passenger who, on one of the *Canberra's* early cruises in 1974, had not realized that the class barriers had come down. Having paid £550 for the most expensive cabin on the ship, he was obviously annoyed to discover that he was getting the same menu as passengers who had paid less than £150. Fortunately, this type of passenger was the exception rather than the rule, and the one-class layout which enabled passengers from the depths of G Deck to enjoy the same facilities as those who occupied the midship suites on C Deck was very popular.

The ship's own daily newspaper, *Canberra News*, provided a summary of world events and then set out the agenda for the day on board; the keep-fit classes, games tournaments, dancing lessons, classical record concerts, fancy dress competitions and port lectures as well as details of duty-free shopping on board. As might be expected many passengers had no need for all this, preferring to relax and contemplate the sea from their deckchairs. There were lunchtime singalongs in the Cricketers' Tavern or ocean-gazing from the panoramic windows of the Crow's Nest. To save fuel the *Canberra* cruised at 18 or 19 knots, her maximum speed being 26 knots, and at the end of the cruise departing passengers disembarked in carefully organized pre-arranged batches and then, less than six hours later, a new company embarked to a completely restocked vessel, spruced to pristine freshness, ready for the whole process to begin all over again.

After carrying out a successful cruising season in 1974 the *Canberra* left Southampton for her 1975 world cruise on 8 January that year. For £993, or the top price of £6,450 if one wanted the best cabin, passengers could escape a grey and grim British winter and enjoy more than 90 days cruising the warmer waters of the Pacific and Indian Oceans on a voyage covering 32,000 miles. The dull, wet day in Southampton Docks was enlivened by the

volunteers from among the passengers to whom he gave full support, and a daily programme was likely to include bingo, the mileage tote, whist drives, chess tournaments, charades and a fancy dress ball, as well as the traditional deck sports. A voyage usually concluded with a passenger concert, backed by a small resident band. The entertainment programmes had changed little since the early 1930s, and for many of the Staff Captains, few of whom had a natural flair for the social side of the job, it was a difficult and thankless task.

Fortunately, it was recognized that professionals would have to be brought in to cater for the cruise passengers who had paid a great deal of money for their holiday, and who were determined to enjoy their short break from what was, perhaps, the humdrum life of office or factory. In the *Canberra* and *Oriana* each ship had two qualified Entertainemnt Officers, six hostesses, three or four professional acts and a star name artiste. There were also three good bands, usually two on a long-term contract and one guest band, plus a port lecturer. With this sort of team and a full cinema listing, high-class professional shows such as revues and cabarets could be put on for the passengers. One cruise director, Bill Johnson, recalls: 'One problem was that of the hostesses. One or two of them came with some show business experience, such as dancing, but on the whole they were social type hostesses, very good for public relations but not suited for stage performances. I suggested to management that if we got six showgirl dancers I could military band and brightly coloured paper streamers which had once made the emigrant departures such poignant affairs, but now the passengers were mainly well-to-do business people, many of whom still missed the exclusiveness of first class travel and complained about the 'types' which the ship tended to attract on different stages of the voyage.

During her 1975 UK cruising season the *Canberra* operated from Southampton in conjunction with the *Arcadia* and the *Oriana*, and this was repeated in 1976. By the autumn of 1976 it was clear that the *Canberra* was firmly established as a very popular cruise ship, and bookings for her 1977, 86-day world cruise were well up on the previous year. This was reflected in the company finances where the figures for that year indicated profits of nearly £1 million would be made following a loss of £6.9 million the previous year. When the *Canberra* left Southampton on 8 January 1977, with 1,200 passengers embarked, it was the only sailing of its kind that year and with fares ranging from £1,187 to £7,171, a spokesman for the Passenger Division commented, 'More people are spending their retirement money and maturing insurance policies on a world cruise. They believe that they should spend it now before inflation reduces its value and puts that long-awaited dream cruise out of their reach.'

One of the high points on the world cruise was the *Canberra's* arrival at Sydney in mid-February. According to one Customs official, whose launch would reach Sydney Heads shortly before 5am on the morning of her arrival, 'Already a golden glow was visible over the South Head and a minute or so later the *Canberra* rounded the headland into Sydney Harbour, lit up like a Christmas tree.' Ten minutes later the launch would run alongside the great white liner and 12 feet above the waterline a brightly lit doorway revealed crew members waiting to receive the officials. As the launch ran smoothly beside the liner, Customs Officers would scramble up the waiting rope ladder with the ease which is only gained from long practice and once on board they would be met by the Deputy Purser who would conduct them to the Crystal Room where, over coffee and biscuits, they could inspect the passenger list. After a short break the officers would be shown to the ship's lounges where disembarking passengers had already formed queues to begin their immigration procedures.

By the time the sun was up, *Canberra* would have berthed at the Sydney Cove Passenger Terminal and ship-to-shore access tunnels would be in position. All the heavy baggage belonging to disembarking passengers would have been unloaded and placed in the Passenger Terminal and by 9am most of them would be on their way to destinations in New South Wales and beyond, while the transit passengers who were taking shore excursions would be preparing to board their coaches on the quayside. As far as the passengers were concerned everything went smoothly and quickly

A bow view of the ship in dry dock with both anchors and their chains having been lowered for maintenance work.
(Vosper Thorneycroft Ltd)

while the port authorities had only a few days' break before the *Oriana* arrived, usually carrying over 1,000 passengers, most of whom would disembark in Sydney.

Following what was usually at least 24 hours in the port the *Canberra* would depart to continue her voyage. If she was eastbound she would steam on to New Zealand, the West Coast of the USA and return home by way of Panama. The westbound journey took her to the Far Eastern ports before returning to the UK via Cape Town. On the completion of her world cruise *Canberra* would arrive back in Southampton in early April, ready to commence her summer cruising season from the port.

When the UK seasonal cruise programme was published for 1977 the *Arcadia* was not included and the *Canberra* and the *Oriana* were to represent the company with a series of 28 cruises to destinations in South America, the Caribbean, Madeira and the Canaries, the Mediterranean and the Norwegian Fjords. The two ships were to set the pattern for P&O cruises which would continue, with only a short break, for 20 years. The cruises ranged from a

The *Canberra* at anchor in Gibraltar Bay with a tender from the port alongside her. *(Mike Lennon)*

seven-day holiday to Madeira and Vigo, to a 24-day voyage to Las Palmas, Tenerife, Rio de Janeiro and Salvador.

On Saturday 30 June 1979 the *Canberra* was in New York as part of a three-week cruise to ports on the east coast of the USA, when she took part in the city's 'Harbor Festival 1979'. At noon that day a grand parade of ships took place in the Hudson River, when the US Coastguard's square-rigger *Eagle* sailed from just off West 79th Street to the Lower Bay as the official lead ship for the vessels from the US Navy, the Coastguard and the Army Corps of Engineers, followed by cargo ships and cruise liners. The *Canberra* had arrived in New York at 8am on Thursday 28 June for a stay of 59 hours and at 7pm on 30 June she left the berth to join the parade of cruise ships, which included the *Rotterdam*, *Statendam*, *Oceanic* and *Doric*. The parade was also joined by numerous tugs, ferries, fire boats and pleasure craft, which made it a day to remember for the *Canberra's* passengers. Ahead of them lay a six-day Atlantic crossing during which they could rest and recuperate before arriving home in Southampton on the morning of Saturday 7 July.

During her 1980 cruising season P&O introduced the idea of 'theme' cruises, with guest celebrities who were able to host such activities as sequence dancing, floral art, bridge classes and even golf with professionals such as Ken

Adwick. These cruises were extremely successful and during the 1980s they would become even more popular as more 'themes' were offered. On her return to Southampton on Sunday 30 November 1980, from an autumn cruise to South America, the *Canberra* was taken over by Vosper Shiprepairers for her annual overhaul, during which she was dry docked and fitted with newly designed propellers and new combustion equipment which would enable her to save on fuel costs. With her dry docking completed the liner was moved to 106 berth in Southampton's Western Docks where Vosper Shiprepairers continued their finishing-off work ready for the *Canberra's* return to service with a Christmas and New Year cruise on Friday 19 December. This was always a popular, well-booked cruise which took passengers to Dakar on Christmas Eve, with calls at Las Palmas and Tenerife and Funchal, Madeira, for New Year's Eve. At 10pm that evening the *Canberra* slipped from her berth in Funchal Harbour and for over three hours she stood off the town to give all the passengers a grandstand view of Madeira's traditional 'Festival of Fireworks' - an unforgettable way of seeing in the New Year. The cruise ended on the morning of Sunday 4 January 1981 and three days later, when she left a very grey and misty Solent for her world cruise with 1,400 passengers embarked, P&O had reason to feel confident, for even though the UK economy was in recession, it was clear that P&O Cruises would remain profitable.

During the 90-day cruise there was much change in the passenger list, with some people leaving and others embarking during the various sectors of the voyage. On 3 March 1981, when *Canberra* called at Hong Kong, many of the passengers made a two-day tour to the People's Republic of China, which was an extremely unusual event in the early 1980s, while others set off on a four-day trip to Bangkok and rejoined the *Canberra* when she docked at Singapore's Keppel Harbour on 9 March. Captain Michael Bradford, who commanded the liner on the Sydney-Southampton sector remarked, 'It was a superb cruise, with beautiful weather practically all the way.' The only scheduled call which had been missed was at Hilo in the Pacific where it was too windy to operate the landing launches. During the cruise a record number of 3,700 passengers had been carried and 28 different nationalities were represented among the 1,650 passengers who were on board for the final leg of the cruise to Southampton.

As always the world cruise was an enormous success, but on her arrival back at Southampton on Wednesday 8 April 1981 to prepare for her UK cruise season, there was industrial trouble brewing at Southampton Docks which would cause a great deal of disruption to a number of cruises. The dispute was over a pay agreement and shift working, but, fortunately, it did not affect holidaymakers on the first cruise which was a 20-day voyage into the Mediterranean calling at Gibraltar, Messina, Haifa, Limassol, Piraeus and Palma, and *Canberra* left on schedule during the evening of Sunday 12 April. However, on Friday 1 May, the day before the cruise ended, the dockers at Southampton decided to work only from 8am to 5pm, Monday to Friday. The first big trial of strength for both workers and management was clearly going to be the *Canberra's* arrival early on the morning of Saturday 2 May. P&O made a special request to the union for a gang of dockers to handle the stores for the liner, but the special payment which was demanded was too high and the company refused to pay it. However, the dockers had not only demanded a highly inflated sum of money, but they also made it clear that, if refused, they would disrupt the liner's arrival and departure.

On the morning of Saturday 2 May all gates in Southampton's Western Docks were closed and locked, primarily to prevent militant dock workers from getting in to picket the *Canberra*, and enormous traffic queues built up on the approach roads near the Post House Hotel and the city's Central Railway Station. As it transpired, the precautions were fully justified, for a large number of pickets would have attempted to physically prevent the berthing of the *Canberra* and with such a large ship committed to the navigable channel, safety was of the utmost importance. The vessel had the assistance of tugs to help her turn before going alongside, and as the first mooring line was secured by P&O officials it appeared that everything would go to plan. Unfortunately, it soon became apparent that if other mooring lines were secured then P&O's entire cargo operation and all its cross-Channel ferries would be brought to a standstill indefinitely. Faced with this it was decided to send the ship to Spithead where the passengers would be ferried ashore to Portsmouth. This decision did not prevent some angry scenes which occurred at Southampton when irate passengers threw apples and other fruit at the few pickets who had got to the quayside in the Western Docks. After anchoring at Spithead three local ferries were hired and the 1,600 passengers were brought into Portsmouth's Camber Docks in batches of 200. As soon as they had disembarked another 1,400 passengers who had been brought by road from Southampton, together with their baggage, were embarked in the same manner. It was an enormous operation, but it was successfully completed and, although it was later than scheduled, Captain Michael Bradford was able to take *Canberra* on her 13-night cruise to the Canary Islands.

The Atlantic Islands cruise finished early on Friday 15 May and there were no problems with her next cruise starting on the same day, although P&O brought forward her departure time to 5pm so that she would not be affected by any industrial action after the ending of the 8am-5pm shift. However, this cruise ended one day early on Friday 22 May so that *Canberra* could complete her turnround within the dockers' permitted hours of working. Passengers on her next cruise to Naples, Dubrovnik, Corfu, Palma and Vigo had an extra 24 hours both at the start and end of their cruise which was due to finish on Sunday 7 June, at no extra cost, but passengers on the following cruise, a 12-night voyage to Vigo, Madeira, Tenerife, Praia da Rocha and Gibraltar, lost one day of their holiday, for which they received a full refund. Fortunately, for everyone concerned, the dispute was settled in mid-July 1981 and all operations by P&O Cruises were able to return to normal. That same month P&O announced that the *Canberra's* cruising season for 1982 would start on 8 April with a nine-night 'sunseekers' cruise to Vigo, Ibiza and Palma, followed by 14 further cruises to destinations ranging from the Italian and French Rivieras, the Algarve, Palma and Sicily, to the Atlantic Islands and the Fjords of Norway.

When the *Canberra* sailed on one of her autumn cruises on Friday 9 October 1981, a 14-day voyage to Gibraltar and the Atlantic Islands, nine stars of screen, radio and sportsfield sailed with her for P&O's third celebrity cruise which was aimed at raising money for the London charitable organization, Lord's Taverners. The line-up included the singer Jess Conrad, comedy scriptwriter Barry Cryer, comedian Harry Worth and comic actor Roy Kinnear, who all guaranteed extra shipboard fun

A beautiful aerial view of the *Canberra* as she steams through the Strait of Gibraltar on a Mediterranean cruise.

(FotoFlite)

An atmospheric view showing the *Canberra* alongside the Overseas Passenger Terminal Sydney.

(P&O)

throughout the cruise. During the fortnight the celebrities entertained passengers by making guest appearances and staging impromptu shows and panel games, as well as deck sports competitions. They also hosted events such as celebrity auctions, sponsored walks, aquatic sports and photo sessions, which not only raised money for the charity but also provided extra entertainment.

Following her late autumn cruise of 17 nights to the Atlantic Islands and Dakar in West Africa, the *Canberra* was once again put into the hands of the Vosper Shiprepairers for her annual overhaul in Southampton's King George V Dry Dock. The work involved the cleaning and painting of the hull, interior refurbishing and machinery maintenance and checks, and once this was completed she was able to leave Southampton on Saturday 12 December 1981 for her 24-night Christmas and New Year cruise. Among the ports on the itinerary were Barbados, Martinique, Port Everglades and Madeira and the liner's 800-strong crew made great efforts to create the festive mood, including fixing a Christmas tree to the mast. Officers sang carols and Father Christmas accompanied

King Neptune to the customary ceremony when the equator was crossed. The *Canberra* returned to Southampton on Tuesday 5 January 1982, and next day at 8pm she left for her 90-day world cruise.

As far as P&O were concerned there was nothing extraordinary about the voyage, apart from the fact that the *Canberra* would spend longer in the Far East and visit more ports in that region than she had ever done before. Fares for the full voyage started at £2,990 for one person in an inside four-berth cabin. The general manager of P&O Cruises commented at the time, 'We are confident that, despite current economic difficulties, there is a strong market for our annual round-the-world cruise, particularly among those for whom this holiday is the realization of a lifelong ambition.'

The company brochure described the cruise as, 'The Voyage Of A Lifetime'. It would certainly be a holiday that her passengers would never forget and before it ended at Southampton on 7 April 1982 the *Canberra* would have been requisitioned for war.

Alongside berth 106 at her home port of Southampton.

(Neil McCart)

Chapter Nine

Preparation For War

At about 11pm on Thursday 1 April 1982, as the *Canberra* steamed through the Ionian Sea between Piraeus and Naples in the final stages of her world cruise, 92 marines of the Argentine Amphibious Commando Company landed on a small unnamed beach near to Lake Point, just two miles south of Stanley, capital of the Falkland Islands, and so set the scene for what will probably be Britain's last colonial conflict.

The dispute between Argentina and Britain over sovereignty of the Falkland Islands and their Dependencies goes back to the last decade of the 17th century when, in 1690, Captain John Strong, who was on a voyage from the UK to Chile, was blown off course and landed on the islands. Whilst provisioning his ship with wild geese and fresh water, Captain Strong charted the sound between the

Massive steel plates are lowered into place over the swimming pool as work continues apace to prepare the ship for the South Atlantic.   *(P&O)*

two main islands, which he named after the First Lord of the Admiralty, Lord Falkland, and then left for Valparaiso. The Argentine claim to the islands stems from the Treaty of Utrecht of 1713 which formally acknowledged Spain's control of its South American territories, which included the Falkland Islands or, as they are known in Spanish, the Islas Malvinas. The first settlement of the islands was made in 1764, in spite of the Treaty of Utrecht, by a French expedition led by Antoine de Bougainville, who built a fort and a small settlement which was called Port Louis, in a position north of what is now Stanley. In the following year Commodore John Byron, who had been sent by the Admiralty to survey the islands, hoisted the Union Flag on West Falkland and it seems he was unaware of the French presence at Port Louis, East Falkland. Commodore Byron did not stay long on the island before returning to Britain, but in 1766 the Government sent out Captain John McBride to consolidate Byron's landing. He was ordered to build a fort and to evict any other occupants of the islands, which resulted in the first contact between the British and the French at the Port Louis settlement, where there were about 250 men.

The Spanish were infuriated that the Treaty of Utrecht was being flagrantly breached by both the French and the British, but as they were allied to the French at that time the settlement was peacefully ceded to Spain with compensation being paid to Antoine de Bougainville and with Port Louis being formally handed over to a Spanish governor, Don Felipe Ruiz Puente, who was appointed by the military governor of Buenos Aires. The handing over ceremony took place in 1767 and two years later, in 1769, the Spanish captain general at Buenos Aires decided to drive the British from Port Egmont and an expedition of 1,500 men was duly sent to carry out the task. Captain George Farmer and his small detachment of marines left the islands under protest and a full-scale diplomatic incident ensued with threats from both sides. Fortunately, an agreement was reached whereby the British detachment was allowed to return to Port Egmont, with Spain keeping sovereignty of both East and West Falkland Islands. However, the British Government made a secret promise to evacuate the settlement, which it did, leaving behind a plaque claiming that the island of West Falkland was: '...the sole right and property of His Most Sacred Majesty George III, King of Great Britain.' The Spanish at Port Soledad (Port Louis) were left in undisputed possession of the islands and, indeed, in 1790 Britain and Spain signed the Nootka Sound Convention by which Britain renounced any colonial

The *Canberra's* profile changes shape as the two flight decks are built and large containers start to fill up the games areas of the Sun Deck.

(P&O)

Men of 40 & 42 Commando Royal Marines, laden with kit and weapons, embark for the voyage south.

(Southern Newspapers Ltd)

The Crow's Nest Bar is stripped of its luxuries and soon the room would be festooned with scaffolding as the forward flight deck is built overhead. *(P&O)*

ambitions in South America and the islands adjacent. This obviously included the Falkland Islands which remained a Spanish colony until the fall of Spain's South American empire in the early part of the 19th century.

In 1810, with nationalist moves towards breaking the ties between Spain and Buenos Aires having started, the Spanish authorities moved the Spanish settlers from Puerto Soledad and from the mainland area of Patagonia. For ten years the Falkland Islands were a refuge for sealing and whaling vessels, but in 1820 the United Provinces of Rio de la Plata, which was the original name of the former Spanish colony and the present day Argentina, sent out a frigate to claim the islands as part of its Spanish legacy. In 1823 the government of Buenos Aires appointed a governor to the islands and in 1829 one of the governors imposed restrictions on the indiscriminate killing of seals which were in danger of extinction, a move which would be applauded today. The only British claim to the islands was a protest from the British Embassy in Buenos Aires at this governor's appointment.

The Argentinian governor Louis Vernet, in his efforts to control the slaughter of seals, arrested an American ship, the *Harriet*, whose captain was sent to Buenos Aires for trial. The US Ambassador in the city arranged for a visiting US Navy warship, the USS *Lexington*, to be sent to Puerto Soledad to recover the sealskins which had been confiscated from the *Harriet*. However, the captain of the *Lexington* went much further than that and he sacked the settlement and arrested most of the inhabitants and declared the islands 'free from all government'. There is no doubt that this action was illegal and another Argentine governor sent to administer the islands was murdered by convicts from a penal colony who had evaded 'arrest' by the captain of the USS *Lexington*.

The British Ambassador in Buenos Aires alerted the Government in London to these events, and in 1833 two Royal Navy warships, HMS *Tyne* and HMS *Clio*, under the command of Captain James Onslow RN, were sent to the islands with instructions from Lord Palmerston to take and to hold the islands for Britain. Antoine de Bougainville had once described his small colony as: '...lifeless for want of inhabitants' and '...everywhere a weird and melancholy uniformity', and with the British Government's decision of 1833 one cannot help but recall the words of a former US President when he said, 'The British would take land anywhere in the world, even if it were only a rock or sandbar.'

Captain Onslow arrived to find Argentine forces hunting down the criminals who had murdered the governor, and they were ordered to lower the Argentine flag and leave. As they were outnumbered and outgunned they did as they were ordered but, in view of the Nootka Sound Convention of 1790, the legality of the British action must be extremely questionable to say the least. However, Captain Onslow then had to take over the hunting down of the bandits who had murdered the previous governor and who refused to accept British sovereignty. One of these individuals, Antonio Rivero, had originally been pursued by the Argentine authorities and when he was finally captured and returned to the South American mainland, he had become a hero.

There is no doubt that had the USS *Lexington* not arbitrarily 'arrested' the inhabitants of Puerto Soledad, then the islands would have remained Argentinian and the British Government would have accepted this fact. However, Britain's occupation of 1833 was to prove more permanent than any previous settlement but, ominously, it was always to be shadowed by the fact that Argentina had persistently claimed sovereignty of the islands, and still does to this day. The strongest British argument rests on the fact that most of the indigenous population wish to remain British, and that the United Nations upholds these wishes. However, Argentina does not recognize this as a valid argument and the dispute over the islands' sovereignty has soured relations between Britain and Argentina since 1833.

For the most part few people in Britain showed any interest in the Falkland Islands, but in December 1914 they were at the centre of world interest when Vice-Admiral Sir Doveton Sturdee, flying his flag in the battlecruiser *Invincible*, and his battle squadron avenged

The midships flight deck provided an ideal area for circuit training as the Royal Marines carried out a relentless programme of physical training during the voyage south.
(Royal Marines Museum)

To an emotional send-off the *Canberra* leaves Southampton for the South Atlantic.
(P&O)

Edinburgh was on an official visit there. As a result of all this, the Royal Marines detachment on the islands, which had been established at platoon strength in 1965 but reduced to six earlier in 1966, was restored to its previous level. In March 1967, during talks between representatives of the Argentine Government and the Foreign and Colonial Secretaries, the British Government, for the first time, indicated that they would be prepared to cede sovereignty over the islands, provided that the wishes of the islanders were respected. There is no doubt that the diplomatic signals which were going out to the Argentine Government indicated that they would succeed eventually in gaining sovereignty. In 1971 agreement was reached with Argentina on a wide range of communication matters, of which the most important was the establishment of an air and sea service between Stanley and Argentina. Other arrangements covered were the provision by Argentina of a 'white card' travel document which guaranteed freedom of movement within Argentina for the islanders, and served in a similar capacity for Argentine citizens travelling to the islands; exemptions from duties and taxes; exemption from Argentine military service for islanders; harmonization of postal and telephone rates; the provision of school places and scholarships in Argentina for the islanders' children; and the establishment of a special consultative committee in Buenos Aires, consisting of the Argentine Foreign Ministry representatives and officials from the British Embassy, to deal with questions arising from the agreement.

the defeat of Coronel by routing Admiral Von Spee's cruiser squadron in the Battle of the Falkland Islands, which took place south-east of Stanley. It was one of the last naval battles to be fought solely by gunfire, without the aid of submarines, aircraft or the threat of minefields. However, this was only a brief moment of glory and thereafter the islands lapsed once again into oblivion with the Second World War largely passing them by, although in December 1939 Stanley provided a haven for Commodore Harwood's cruiser *Exeter* following the damage she received during the Battle of the River Plate.

It was in 1963 that there was a resurgence of Argentine interest in the Falkland Islands and the Government in Buenos Aires instituted a 'Malvinas Day'. In September 1964 an Argentine civilian landed a light aircraft at Stanley, planted an Argentine flag, handed out a proclamation and took off again. Although the Argentine Government dissociated themselves from the incident, they did nothing to deter such exploits and, indeed, they watched the British reaction to them closely. In September 1966 another unofficial incident took place when an armed group of 20 young Argentines hijacked an Argentine Airlines DC4 and forced it to fly to the Falklands where it landed on Stanley racecourse. Once again the Argentine Government dissociated themselves, but there were public demonstrations in towns and cities throughout Argentina in support of the incident, and shots were fired at the British Embassy in Buenos Aires while the Duke of

Following this the Argentine Government continued to press for negotiations on sovereignty and by mid-1973 it was clear that an impasse had been reached. However, in early 1974 it seemed that agreement might be reached with the formation of a condominium, but with the islanders refusing to take part in talks this idea was dropped. In December that year an Argentine newspaper started a campaign advocating a military invasion of the islands, from which, once again, the Government in Buenos Aires only half-heartedly dissociated itself. On 8 December 1975 the Argentine representative at the United Nations made a speech in which he said: 'We are prepared to continue our efforts, but the limits of our patience and tolerance should not be underestimated if we should have to face an

There was still some time for relaxation when, during the evening of Sunday 18 April, the Band of the Royal Marines beat Retreat on the midships flight deck.
(Royal Marines Museum)

The *Canberra's* first port of call on the voyage south was Freetown in Sierra Leone, where she made a stop of just over 12 hours to refuel. She is seen here secured to the Kissy Fuel Jetty.
(P&O)

It's still 'almost' silver service in the Pacific Restaurant. Royal Marines officers at breakfast on the way south. *(Southern Newspapers Ltd)*

In February 1976 an Argentine warship fired shots at the research ship *Shackleton* and unsuccessfully tried to arrest her for an alleged infringement on Argentina's territorial waters. However, as they claimed all the waters within 200 miles of the coast, which included the Falkland Islands, it was clear that the incident was contrived. In response, the British Government stationed the ice-patrol vessel HMS *Endurance* and a Royal Navy frigate in the area. At about the same time the Defence Chiefs of Staff drew up an assessment of what would be required to dislodge a determined Argentine invasion of the islands, which concluded that to recover them by military means, though far from impossible, would involve a major operation at very long range. It would include the use of all the Navy's amphibious resources, and the one remaining fleet aircraft carrier, HMS *Ark Royal*.

In early 1977 it became known that the Argentines had established a military presence in Southern Thule in the South Sandwich Islands. Britain had unilaterally declared sovereignty over these islands in 1908, along with South Georgia, and declared them to be Falkland Islands Dependencies, but apart from a diplomatic protest in Buenos Aires, Britain took no action over the bases. Indeed, it was 1978 before the British public became aware of the Argentine presence. However, it had the effect of saving the ice-patrol ship *Endurance* from being withdrawn as had been intended, and it was clear that the proposed withdrawal was taken by Argentina to be a clear sign that Britain was not seriously interested in her South Atlantic possessions. In late 1979, with the advent of a Conservative Government, Britain was still searching for an agreement with Argentina and one of the options thought possible was a transfer of sovereignty with a leaseback by the islanders. However, when they were consulted, they rejected the idea and suggested that the British Government should seek an agreement to freeze the sovereignty dispute for a specified period of time, but this was rejected outright by the Argentines.

By late 1981 the Argentine Government was complaining about lack of progress with negotiations and their UN representative addressed the General Assembly by

obstinate and unjustified refusal to negotiate by the other party.' Any ambiguities about what was meant were soon dispelled when he concluded the speech by stating: 'The Argentine Government reserves its position regarding the responsibility which rests with the British Government for the breaking-off of negotiations and will not fail to assert its rights in the form which it deems most appropriate.' During 1976 the Argentine press continued to campaign for an invasion of the islands and the British Joint Intelligence Committee concluded that, 'Argentina is unlikely to launch a sudden invasion in the near future...but physical aggression cannot be excluded.'

Canberra refuels from RFA *Plumleaf* off Ascension Island, as seen from the RFA.

(*G. Mortimore/Action Photos*)

A *Plumleaf's* eye view of the *Canberra's* temporary RAS (Replenishment At Sea) point which had been fitted to the Promenade Deck.

(G. Mortimore/Action Photos)

Canberra refuels from RFA *Tidepool.*

(P&O)

HMS *Fearless, Canberra* and other ships of the task force anchored off Ascension Island. *(P&O)*

referring to the, 'present illegal occupation,' of the islands and expressed his Government's hope that they would be, '... able to report in due course to the General Assembly that this series of negotiations concerning the Malvinas, South Georgia and South Sandwich Islands, which we hope will begin soon, was the last one.' During 1981 it had been announced that, as a result of the Defence Review, it had been decided to withdraw the Royal Navy's last presence in the South Atlantic, HMS *Endurance*, and this was confirmed in Parliament on 30 June that year. The announcement was taken by both the Falkland Islands Council and the Argentine Government as a further sign of Britain's diminishing interest in the islands and, indeed, a paper by the Chiefs of Staff that year concluded that, '...to deal with a full-scale invasion would require naval and land forces with organic air support on a very substantial scale, and that the logistic problems of such an operation would be very formidable.' There is no doubt that the scrapping of the Royal Navy's last two big fleet aircraft carriers *Eagle* and *Ark Royal* had given the Argentine military great comfort.

On 22 December 1981, General Leopoldo Galtieri succeeded President Roberto Viola as the President of Argentina, at the same time retaining his position as the C-in-C of the Argentine Army. On 19 January 1982, as the *Canberra* steamed through the Caribbean between Port Everglades and Panama, the Governor of the Falkland Islands noted that the islanders were deeply suspicious of both the British and Argentine Governments and that they were strongly opposed to the idea of leaseback. They were disappointed by the British Government's refusal to grant

them British citizenship, by the proposed withdrawal of the *Endurance* and by the threatened closure of the British Antarctic Survey base at Grytviken, South Georgia. They were even more alarmed by the Argentine Government's reduction in the frequency of the air service to the islands and the fact that Argentine Air Force aircraft had been making what appeared to be reconnaissance flights over the islands.

On 27 January 1982, while the *Canberra* was in the Pacific Ocean, between Acapulco and San Francisco, the Argentine Government delivered a communication to the British Ambassador in Buenos Aires stating that British recognition of Argentine sovereignty over the Malvinas, South Georgia and the South Sandwich Islands remained an essential requirement for the solution of the dispute. It went on to say that however much time might pass, Argentina would never abandon its claim nor relax its determination and it called for serious negotiations which would, 'within a reasonable period of time and without procrastination' result in a recognition of Argentine sovereignty over the disputed islands. It pointed out that the matter had reached a point which, 'demands solutions without further delays or dilatory arguments.' Unfortunately, none of this was taken too seriously by the Foreign Office, although the 150th anniversary of the British occupation of the islands was approaching and the Argentine Government would obviously want the occasion to be marked in a very dramatic way.

By March 1982 the political negotiations which were taking place in New York were overshadowed by events in South Georgia and the actions of a hitherto unknown scrap

The *Canberra* anchored off Ascension Island on 1 May, 1982 as seen from RFA *Plumleaf*.   (*G. Mortimore/Action Photos*)

metal dealer. Constantino Davidoff was a scrap merchant from Buenos Aires who, in 1978, had approached Christian Salveson, the Edinburgh-based company which manages Crown leases for the disused whaling stations on South Georgia. In the following year he signed a contract giving him an option to purchase equipment from the stations, and in 1980 he exercised the option, with any equipment remaining on site after March 1983 reverting to Christian Salveson. Between 1979 and late 1981 Sr Davidoff was in occasional contact with the British Embassy in Buenos Aires, and on 16 December 1981 he left Buenos Aires in the Argentine naval ice-breaker, *Almirante Irizar*, to inspect the scrap on South Georgia. However, the British Embassy in Buenos Aires was not notified until after he had left the city, and only two days before he arrived at Leith on 20 December. On 31 December 1981 the Governor of the Falkland Islands

reported to the Foreign and Commonwealth Office in London the unauthorized presence of the *Almirante Irizar* in Stromness Bay, South Georgia. The governor recommended that proceedings be instituted against Davidoff and a strong diplomatic protest be made to the Argentine Government. However, the Government in London did not wish to provoke the Argentines and it was agreed that if Davidoff reported to the British Antarctic Survey at Grytviken and requested entry permits for himself and the naval vessel, then it would be granted. On 9 February 1982 the British Ambassador in Buenos Aires lodged a formal protest with the Argentine Government at the breach of sovereignty, but this was rejected by the Foreign Ministry in Buenos Aires. It was clear that the Argentines were testing British reactions to their aggression and, unfortunately, the signals they were receiving appeared to confirm their suspicions that the British Government took no interest in its South Atlantic possessions.

Two weeks later, on 28 February 1982, Sr Davidoff visited the British Embassy in Buenos Aires where he apologized for the problems caused by his visit to South Georgia and announced that he wished to make another visit to the island. He was clearly anxious not to cause any more international incidents and he asked for full instructions on how to proceed. Unfortunately, there was a delay on the British side and by the time of his group's departure on 11 March, in the Argentine naval support vessel *Bahia Buen Sucesco*, he had received no reply. On Friday 19 March, as the *Canberra* lay at anchor off Port Victoria in the Seychelles, the British Antarctic Survey members saw the *Bahia Buen Sucesco* anchored in Leith Harbour, with a sizeable party of her crew members ashore. In addition to this, shots had been heard and an Argentine flag had been raised on an improvised flagpole. Although the incidents could possibly have been carried out spontaneously, it was strongly suspected that Sr Davidoff's party was being used as a front to challenge British authority, particularly as they had ignored instructions to obtain landing permits from the British magistrate at Grytviken. It was agreed in London that HMS *Endurance* should sail for South Georgia with a detachment of marines on board to evict the Argentines.

On Monday 22 March the *Bahia Buen Sucesco* left Leith and on the same day the Governor of the Falkland Islands telegraphed London to say that Sr Davidoff's party was deliberately flouting the British regulations and that more illegal landings were likely, probably on the Falkland Islands themselves. On the following day the matter was raised in the House of Commons and over the next two days diplomatic relations between London and Buenos Aires deteriorated rapidly. By Thursday 25 March, as the *Canberra* steamed up the Red Sea towards Suez, information was received in London that Argentine warships were being sent to South Georgia to prevent HMS *Endurance* from evicting the Argentines there, and to intercept the British ship between South Georgia and the Falkland Islands. It was also learned that another Argentine naval supply ship, the *Bahia Paraiso*, had arrived at Leith and was working cargo, and in addition to this three landing craft and a military helicopter were operating from the vessel. It was also reported that the *Bahia Paraiso* was flying the flag of the Argentine Navy's Senior Officer, Antarctic Squadron. In London it was feared that any attempt to resolve the situation effectively would result in a full-scale military action by Argentina, and so further diplomatic efforts were made to persuade the Argentines to remove the men.

On Saturday 27 March, with the *Canberra* having completed her Suez Canal transit and whilst she was moored at Port Said, it became clear that there was intense naval activity at the Argentine bases in Mar del Plata and Puerto Belgrano, with the embarkation of marines and the sailing of several ships. Next day, as the *Canberra* visited the port of Haifa, Argentina's Foreign Minister made it clear that the Argentines at South Georgia would remain on the island and that the blame for the existing situation lay with Britain for not accepting Argentinian sovereignty. By midday on Monday 29 March, when the *Canberra* was steaming through the Mediterranean Sea between Haifa and Piraeus, the British Naval Attache in Buenos Aires reported to London that five Argentine warships, including a submarine, were sailing to South Georgia, and that another four warships, including the aircraft carrier, *Vienticinco de Mayo*, were also at sea. There were also reports that travel restrictions had been imposed on Argentine military personnel at their bases. It was immediately recognized by the Ministry of Defence that the presence of Argentine ships at sea some 800 miles north of the Falkland Islands, as well as warships close to South Georgia, was a highly unusual situation, and it was decided to dispatch three nuclear-powered submarines to the South Atlantic. Consideration was also given to the question of a larger naval force, should it be required.

By the evening of Wednesday 31 March, as the *Canberra* was preparing to leave Piraeus for Naples, her final port of call on her 90-day world cruise, reliable intelligence reports indicated that the Argentine armed forces were set to invade both the Falkland Islands and South Georgia. This information was immediately relayed to the Governor of the Falkland Islands and there was frantic diplomatic activity in an effort to head off the invasion. However, it was all in vain, for the Argentine invasion plans had been first hatched in December 1981 and no diplomatic manoeuvrings, however skilful, would deflect the Argentine Military Junta from its purpose. So, at 11pm local time on Thursday 1 April 1982, Argentine marines of the elite Amphibious Commando Company left the British designed, type 42 destroyer *Santissima Trinidad*, which was anchored a mile off the coast of East Falkland, to attack the empty Royal Marines barracks at Moody Brook. Next morning, at 6.30am, as the *Canberra* approached Naples, the main Argentine force landed just north of Stanley and by 8am, as *Canberra's* mooring lines were secured, the Argentinians had taken possession of the islands' capital, Stanley, and were attacking Government House. It did not take the huge Argentine invasion force long to overwhelm the garrison of 80 Royal Marines and by 9.30am that morning they were in control of the islands. However, in the UK an unprecedented national sense of shock and outrage was being expressed and it was quickly decided to send a large task force to the South Atlantic to retake the islands for Britain.

It seemed simple enough to announce the dispatch of a task force, but assembling the huge armada of warships, troop transports and supply vessels to sail 8,000 miles to

The *Canberra* in San Carlos Water as helicopters provided a shuttle service to fly stores ashore. *(P&O)*

the South Atlantic posed huge logistical problems for the service chiefs. Another major problem was that of air cover, as the Royal Navy's big fleet aircraft carriers *Eagle* and *Ark Royal* with their formidable strike power and AEW capability, had been scrapped in the 1970s leaving only the *Hermes* and the *Invincible* which, even if loaded to capacity, could carry only a fraction of the aircraft which a fleet carrier could embark. Sadly, the RAF's boast that they could provide all Britain's air defence requirements had proved to be totally hollow and it was obvious that the Navy was the only service which would be able to provide air cover for a landing force. The amphibious assault group which would be required to carry the troops to the South Atlantic and to supply them would require the immediate requisitioning of merchant ships of all types, and during the afternoon of 2 April P&O staff were called to the Ministry of Defence to discuss the requirements with Government officials. It was at this meeting that it became clear that the *Canberra* would be requisitioned as a troop transport and, in fact, when the liner left Naples at about midnight on 2/3 April, the meetings were still in session.

During the morning of Saturday 3 April, at his home in Worcester, Captain Michael Bradford, one of the *Canberra's* senior masters, received a call to go to Plymouth where he was to join an advanced planning party who would fly out to *Canberra* whilst she was on her way home, and at 9pm on Sunday 4 April the liner made an unscheduled stop in Gibraltar Bay to embark them. Meanwhile, that same evening, Captain Scott-Masson, the *Canberra's* master, was officially informed that the ship was to be requisitioned by the MoD. It was just over 33 years since the *Strathnaver* had become the last of P&O's liners to be released from government service following her requisition during the Second World War, and in August 1939, a week before the outbreak of war, the P&O liner *Rawalpindi* was one of the first merchant ships to be requisitioned on receipt of a telegram reading, 'Your vessel *Rawalpindi* is hereby requisitioned for government service.' Over 42 years later, on Monday 5 April 1982, P&O's formal notification came by letter from the Department of Trade, addressed to Mr Alan Langley, Operations Director of P&O Cruises. The first paragraph read: 'The Secretary of State for Trade in

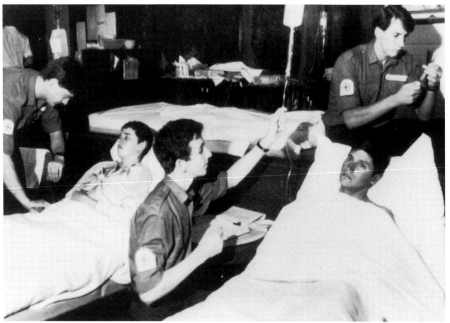

Casualties, both British and Argentinian, are treated in the *Canberra's* hospital.
(P&O)

exercising the powers conferred upon him by the Requisitioning of Ships Order 1982 hereby requisitions the SS *Canberra* and requires you to place the said vessel at his disposal forthwith. The vessel should proceed immediately to Southampton Berth 105.' Which was, of course, where the *Canberra* was heading anyway.

That same day the two aircraft carriers *Hermes* and *Invincible*, together with the assault ship *Fearless*, sailed from Portsmouth in a blaze of publicity and amid scenes of emotion designed to show Argentina's military leaders that Britain meant business. As the naval task force left Portsmouth, the *Canberra* steamed north at 23 knots off the coast of Portugal, and at 7.30am on Wednesday 7 April, right on schedule, she was secured alongside 105 berth of Southampton's Western Docks, her world cruise at an end and her government service about to begin.

Already *Canberra's* first five cruises of her UK cruising season had been cancelled and notices sent to would-be passengers, many of whom had booked their holiday the previous year. The first of these cruises was a nine-night voyage to Vigo and the Balearic Islands which had been scheduled to start on the evening of Thursday 8 April and it was important that intending passengers be notified not to turn up at Southampton Docks. The other four cruises were two-week holidays to the Atlantic Islands and Mediterranean ports which took the ship's schedule through to Mid-June, beyond which nobody at that time could foresee.

Less than two hours after having berthed at

Southampton the *Canberra's* world cruise passengers started to disembark and by noon, as the workforce of Vospers Shiprepairers converged on the ship, they were clear of the docks. Plans had been hurriedly prepared to fit the liner with helicopter flight decks, one forward of the bridge superstructure above the Crow's Nest and Stadium and the second amidships on the Sun Deck above the Bonito Pool. Both flight decks had to be supported by steel girders and some of those used amidships actually stood in the Bonito Pool. Below decks the shops and even the ladies hairdressing salon were stripped for use as offices, and huge quantities of hardboard were laid down in alleyways and in public rooms in order to protect the carpets. Almost immediately large sections of the ship's guard rail and the windbreaks from the midships section of the Sun Deck were cut away and piled up on the quayside in great heaps of tangled metal. Large sections of steel plate had already begun to arrive, and work on the midships flight deck proceeded quickly. However, the sheer quantities of steel plate required indicated that the work would not be completed on Thursday 8 April, and sailing was postponed for 24 hours. At noon on Wednesday the embarkation of troops began, with the Royal Marines of 40 and 42 Commando and men of the Third Parachute Regiment going on board, together with a number of supporting units. Altogether the *Canberra* would carry approximately 2,500 troops to the South Atlantic and the embarkation was well summed up by the Regimental Sergeant Major who appeared on television news bulletins the world over ordering his men to embark with the command, '...To the South Atlantic, Up the gangway, Quick march!'

Once the embarkation was completed Captain Scott-Masson welcomed the men on board and part of his speech is worth recording here: 'Now that embarkation is complete, I should like to welcome you on board P&O's SS *Canberra*. This is an unusual role for this ship and we hope you will be as happy as the passengers that we normally carry - but of course with the added advantage that you are not paying for it. The P&O has a long history of association with Her Majesty's Services and we are delighted to welcome on board the Third Battalion, the Parachute Regiment. 40-42 Commando and all the embarked services personnel. We believe this voyage to the sunshine cruising area, for which we are well adapted, will provide a unique experience for those on board. Nobody knows exactly what the future holds for us, but I have no doubt that working together we shall accomplish everything that is asked of us and, believe me, you have the full support of all the ship's company which I command. It has been most encouraging to receive an enormous amount of good wishes for the unusual deployment that we are about to embark on. You have all had time to notice a few printed "Welcomes on board" and I quote: "P&O Sunshine Cruises Welcomes 40-42 Commando, Third Paras, across the Atlantic with dry feet courtesy of the *Canberra*", and this includes all other personnel embarked.'

Throughout the evening and night of 8/9 April work continued, under the glare of powerful arc lights, to complete the flight decks and, finally, by 8pm on the evening of Friday 9 April the *Canberra* was ready for sea. All that day the radio and television news reporters had speculated on the time of her sailing and by 5pm that evening thousands of people had gathered in the city's Mayflower Park, on Town Quay and all along Hythe shoreline to watch the great liner depart. She was to leave in a blaze of media publicity, and after all the misunderstandings and failures of diplomacy on both sides there was to be no ambiguity about the sailing of the *Canberra* and her mission - she was bound for the South Atlantic, packed with some of Britain's best military units and they 'meant business'.

At 8.15pm that evening, as darkness fell, all lines were clear and the ship was pulled slowly from her berth as the band of the Parachute Regiment played and hundreds of relatives on the quayside bade her farewell. Half a mile down Southampton Water the vessel passed close by the city's Mayflower Park, which on the evening of that warm Good Friday public holiday was packed with thousands of well-wishers. With the troops manning the decks and standing to attention, the ship's siren boomed out, and the crowd replied with a spontaneous cacophony of cheering and car horns amid a blaze of headlights. Half an hour later the deep boom of the ship's siren could be heard as she turned into the Solent and round the Isle of Wight.

The P&O chairman, Lord Inchcape, sent the following message to Captain Scott-Masson: 'As *Canberra* takes her place in the Falkland Islands task force, your colleagues elsewhere in the fleet, and ashore the world over, go with you in spirit. You and your ship's company may count upon our total support. Whatever its outcome, your present enterprise must take a prominent place in the annals of the company and, indeed, in the history of the nation. With you, we pray that its progress may be peaceful, and its objectives successfully won. We, every one of us, wish you God Speed and safe return.'

The *Canberra's* next 94 days would not be peaceful, but the objectives would be successfully won.

The *Canberra* at anchor off Grytviken, South Georgia.

(P&O)

Chapter Ten

Hostile Waters And Home Again

After leaving Southampton the *Canberra* rendezvoused with the MV *Elk*, a P&O roll-on/roll-off ferry, and the Royal Fleet Auxiliary (RFA) *Plumleaf*, and by noon on 10 April the three ships had been joined by a Soviet spy vessel, which stayed in close attendance until they reached Ascension Island. That same day a Sea King helicopter from RNAS Culdrose landed on *Canberra's* midships flight deck, the first of many such landings, and the embarked troops were drilled in General Emergency Stations for the first time. On Monday 12 April RFA *Plumleaf* manoeuvred alongside the liner and mail was transferred by light jackstay, the exercise providing a practice run for the forthcoming RAS (Refuelling At Sea), which the *Canberra* would of necessity have to carry out at regular intervals.

As the *Canberra* steamed south, diplomatic efforts, in conjunction with the American envoy Alexander Haig, took on a new urgency but with no compromise on either side it was becoming clear that the military solution would prevail. By Thursday 15 April the *Canberra* was off Dakar in West Africa and her decks resounded to the thundering of hundreds of pounding feet as the relentless training programmes ensured that troops kept as fit as was possible in such confined spaces. Two days later, at 8am on Saturday 17 April, *Canberra* anchored in the approaches to Freetown, Sierra Leone, prior to entering the harbour three hours later for refuelling. As the great ship took on fuel, fresh water and various other stores, local bum-boats approached and had to be repelled. At midnight the *Canberra* left Freetown and resumed her voyage south.

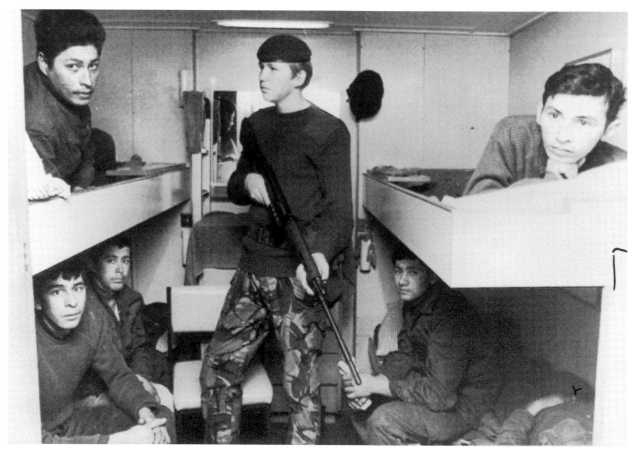

Argentine prisoners under guard in one of *Canberra's* four-berth cabins. No early morning tea was being served.   *(P&O)*

During the evening of 18 April another 'first' took place when the band of the Royal Marines impressively Beat Retreat on the midships flight deck, with the salute being taken by Captain Dennis Scott-Masson. That night, with no ceremony, Canberra crossed the equator and on the next day, Monday 19 April, came the order to 'darken ship' - a highly unusual situation for this passenger ship which was designed to be floodlit at sea and in ports the world over.

At 7.35am on Tuesday 20 April the Canberra anchored just half a mile west of Pyramid Point in the north-west of Ascension Island. This lonely Atlantic outpost, administered from St Helena, is a satellite tracking station with a small settlement at Georgetown and a long airfield known as Wideawake Airstrip, which is used mainly by the US Air Force. The island itself is volcanic in origin and also happens to be the nesting place of a particularly rare breed of Sooty Tern. For the Canberra and her embarked troops, however, it was to be a welcome break and an opportunity for landing exercises and weapons training in albeit hot, dusty conditions which would be very different from those which they would encounter further south.

After two days at anchor Canberra put to sea on the morning of Thursday 22 April to carry out RAS trials with the RFA Pearleaf. However, no sooner had these got under way than she was recalled to the anchorage to embark two personnel who had been injured during exercises, and for the rest of that day and the following day ammunition and stores were embarked by helicopter. During the morning of Sunday 25 April the 10,409-gross ton Argentine cargo ship, Rio de la Plata, which was owned by the Empress Lineas Maritimas Argentinas SA but, in effect, controlled by the Argentine Government Shipping Department, was found to be sailing close to the island. The Type 21 frigate HMS Antelope was sent to clear her from the area and to

ensure that she did not return. That same day came the news that the Argentine submarine Santa Fe had been attacked and disabled, and the island of South Georgia had been regained which, although it served to boost morale, meant little in strategic terms. The very presence of the Argentine cargo ship so close to the ships assembled off Ascension Island led to fears of an underwater attack and from that day onwards, whilst the Canberra was off Ascension, she put to sea every evening and anchored once more the following morning.

The Canberra remained in the vicinity of Ascension Island until the afternoon of Thursday 6 May when, in company with the Elk, RFA Tidepool and the frigates Argonaut and Ardent, she weighed anchor and set course south. By this time, in the vicinity of the Falkland Islands, aircraft and warships of the task force were carrying out a continual bombardment and shelling of Argentine positions. Any doubts about the nature of the conflict had been dispelled with the sinking of the cruiser General Belgrano and the destroyer HMS Sheffield which had been crippled by an air-launched Exocet missile. It was clear to all aboard Canberra that, not only was the campaign becoming very dangerous, but that a landing on hostile shores was now almost a certainty and air raid alerts became second nature. By mid-May the Canberra was some 800 miles east-north-east of the Falkland Islands and into the stormy ocean tracts between latitudes 40° and 50° south, known as the Roaring Forties, where she was met by gale force winds and heavy seas, and two days later she was within 100 miles of the Total Exclusion Zone (TEZ), which had been declared around the islands. By now a number of general-purpose machine-guns had been secured to the Canberra's guard rails in order to provide anti-aircraft fire and these were now manned in earnest during the air raid warnings which were becoming more frequent as the ship moved closer to the islands. Down below in the liner the Stadium was prepared for use as an operating theatre for, following the disembarkation and landing of her troops, she had been designated to act as a casualty clearing centre as well as a rest and recuperation area and a reserve force ship.

On Wednesday 19 May the *Canberra* was just over 230 miles from Stanley, and with the deadly efficiency of the Argentine Air Force having become apparent, orders were received to transfer 1,200 men to the two naval assault ships, HMS *Fearless* and HMS *Intrepid*, which, with a heavy sea swell running, was no easy task. However, between 9.30am and 11am, men of 40 Commando Royal Marines undertook the jump from the *Canberra's* gunport door into an LCU which was pitching heavily on the swell, in order that they could be transferred to the much less comfortable assault ships. Fortunately, the operation was completed successfully with no loss of life, and with only one man misjudging the distance and ending up in the icy cold waters of the Southern Ocean. It was clear that the main

landings of British forces onto the Falkland Islands were imminent, and that evening Colonel T. Seccombe RM, the Military Force Commander, brought everyone on board up to date with events as they related to the *Canberra*.

In the early hours of Thursday 20 May, the *Canberra* and the other vessels of the assault convoy, escorted by HM Ships *Antrim*, *Brilliant*, *Broadsword*, *Yarmouth*, *Ardent*, *Argonaut* and *Plymouth*, with the *Invincible* providing air cover, set course west for the north entrance to Falkland Sound. That evening the assault force formed into three waves, with the two naval assault ships, *Fearless* and *Intrepid*, and the *Canberra*, escorted by HM Ships *Plymouth* and *Brilliant*, making up the first wave. At 10.12pm, having rounded Cape Dolphin, they formed line ahead and at 11pm the liner commenced her passage into Falkland Sound to take up an overnight anchorage off Fanning Head. Despite the fact that darkness had fallen, these were tense hours and with the ship at General Emergency Stations the *Canberra* anchored at 17 minutes past midnight on the morning of 21 May, or D-Day. During the early hours troops disembarked from various

During the *Canberra's* voyage home there was much more time for relaxation and the Royal Marines Band were able to entertain the embarked troops.

(*Royal Marines Museum*)

Above: As the *Canberra* nears the end of her long voyage, small boats escort her back into the Solent on what was to be a gloriously sunny day.
(*P&O*)

Right: On the morning of Sunday 11 July, as the *Canberra* entered the Solent for her triumphant homecoming, HRH The Prince of Wales flew on board to meet members of the ship's company. Here he meets Chef Denis Rogers who was due to retire as soon as the ship arrived alongside.
(*The News, Portsmouth*)

ships in order to deal with Argentine forces on Fanning Head, and at 5.20am the *Canberra* weighed anchor to make the 45-minute passage into San Carlos Water, where she anchored at 6.05am.

At dawn that morning, an Argentine Army lookout went to high ground overlooking San Carlos Water and, to his amazement, he saw the huge white liner steaming to her anchorage no more than three miles away from the hillside where he was watching through his binoculars. Soon afterwards, when the morning mist had cleared, he saw the screen of warships and the first of many landing craft leaving the side of the *Canberra* for the shore. Then, before many more minutes had passed, he saw landing craft travelling in all directions, and columns of troops advancing up the hillsides towards the settlement of San Carlos. 'Operation Sutton', the British landings, had begun.

Although the Argentine lookout had been unable to prevent the landings, the officer in charge of his patrol, Lieutenant Esteban, immediately reported what was clearly a major troop landing to his headquarters at Goose Green, and it was not long before the Argentine Air Force mounted the first of many formidable attacks on the invasion force, including the *Canberra*.

The first of the air attacks on the shipping in San Carlos Water came at just before 9am that day in the form of a Pucara aircraft which fired rockets at both the *Argonaut* and the *Canberra*, before it was shot down by anti-aircraft fire. Soon after that two Mirage jets made a low-level attack, followed by further waves of both Mirage and Skyhawk aircraft. It was during this attack that HMS *Antrim* was hit by a bomb which did not explode, but it did disable her missile systems. Of necessity the Argentine Air Force had to make very low level attacks in the sheltered waters of San Carlos Water, which was protected by the surrounding hills, and their bomb fuses did not have time to arm themselves before they hit their targets. At this time the *Canberra* also came under attack and her air defence teams blazed away with their machine-guns, while the Argentine pilots must have considered the liner an easy target as they roared over the massive white ship. On the bridge the liner's Senior Naval Officer (SNO) kept up a calm commentary over the ship's tannoy system, which did a great deal to reassure those who were down below and who could hear the dreadful din, but had little idea of what was happening.

The main Argentine air attacks were spread over a period of about six hours and the aircraft came in over the anchorage in waves of between five and 14 aircraft at roughly half hour intervals. As far as the *Canberra* was concerned it was imperative that the troops on board be disembarked as quickly as possible, and at just after 10am 42 Commando Royal Marines started to disembark into LCUs, an operation that went on all day and well into the evening, even during the air attacks. Early that same afternoon the frigate HMS *Ardent* was hit and seriously

damaged by bombs and the survivors, who were taken off by HMS *Yarmouth*, were embarked in the *Canberra*. That evening, at 10.42pm, with the last of the troops having been disembarked, the liner weighed anchor and left the Falkland Sound for an area 130 miles north-north-east of the islands. She also had on board 21 casualties, three of whom were Argentinians. On Friday 21 May, during the relentless air attacks which were pressed home with fierce determination, and resisted equally fiercely by the ships' companies of the frigates and destroyers, *Canberra* was affectionately nicknamed 'the Great White Whale' for, to observers ashore, she appeared to be just that as enemy aircraft rushed overhead.

Next day, in a position Lat 51° - 01'S/Long 54° - 43'W the bodies of four crew members of a Gazelle helicopter, which had been shot down during the morning of D-Day, were committed to the deep. The *Canberra* spent one more full day in the area, during which she embarked casualties before, at 1.36pm on Tuesday 25 May, she set course with the MV *Norland* for South Georgia.

Two weeks earlier, on Monday 10 May, the *QE2* which had also been requisitioned by the Government, sailed from Southampton with military reinforcements in the form of the Fifth Infantry Brigade. Because her arrival in the vicinity of the Falkland Islands would have coincided with the Argentine National Day, it had been decided to transfer the men to the *Canberra* and the *Norland* in the relative safety of the harbour of Grytviken in South Georgia. During the early hours of Thursday 27 May the two ships were forced to reduce speed when icebergs were sighted and because of their abundance, 'ice lookouts' were stationed on the bridge wings. At 1.15pm that day the *Canberra* anchored in East Cumberland Bay, Grytviken, to await the arrival of the *QE2* and almost seven hours later, having been delayed by ice and poor visibility, the great Cunarder arrived. That same night the transfer of the troops and their stores and equipment began. Meanwhile, to the west the campaign had continued with the commencement of the two-day battle for Goose Green, with the main action being fought on Friday 28 May followed by the surrender of the Argentine Garrison at just before noon on 29 May. The Argentine commander at Stanley had been given a crushing demonstration of Britain's determination to retake the islands.

At Grytviken, Friday 28 May proved to be a very busy day for the *Canberra's* ship's company as the embarkation of troops and stores continued, and the survivors from HMS *Ardent* were transferred to the *QE2* for the voyage home to Southampton. This was an emotional occasion and all *Canberra's* crew and the Royal Marines Band turned out to bid them farewell. Finally, at 8.50pm *Canberra* weighed anchor and set course for San Carlos Water once more. At the time there was a good deal of criticism that the *QE2* had not been allowed to steam into San Carlos Water

A magnificent stern view of the *Canberra* as she steams through the Solent. Already the small boats have started to surround her.

(*Mike Lennon*)

The Royal Marines Band and Naval Party 1071 have pride of place on the forward flight deck as the *Canberra* steams up Southampton Water.
(Royal Marines Museum)

herself but, in view of the devastating efficiency of the Argentine Air Force and the fact that it was well known that they still had a number of air-launched Exocet missiles left, it was a wise decision. The destruction of the Cunarder, which was generally considered to be the flagship of the Mercantile Marine, would have been a blow to the morale of both the British troops and to the public at home.

On Saturday 29 May, as the *Canberra* steamed through foul weather and heavy seas towards the Falkland Islands, air defence crews and the Royal Navy fire parties were exercised but, of course, the main worry concerned the Super Etendards and their Exocet missiles which could be launched with deadly accuracy from more than 30 miles away. Having been deprived of its AEW aircraft in the late 1970s, there is no doubt that the task force, and the Navy's two aircraft carriers in particular, keenly felt the lack of AEW capability. During the morning of Monday 31 May the *Canberra* rendezvoused with the carriers *Hermes* and *Invincible* and early on the morning of 2 June she entered

the Falkland Sound once again. Fortunately, it was a dull and foggy morning, and so thick was the fog that no helicopters could fly, which provided ideal conditions for those on board the *Canberra*, and at 6.30am that morning the disembarkation of the Scots and Welsh Guards began. Later in the day, as work continued to transfer troops and stores, the fog lifted to reveal a clear and sunny afternoon which gave a new urgency to complete the task and get the *Canberra* back to sea once again. Although the troops and their equipment had been disembarked by the evening, some stores remained on board and it was decided that, despite the danger from air attack, the *Canberra* would have to remain at the anchorage until everything had been unloaded.

During Thursday 3 June the 'Great White Whale', as she had become affectionately known, lay at her anchorage in San Carlos Water as the unloading of her stores continued and, once again, her luck held. By 6pm that evening the task was completed and under the cover of the very welcome darkness the *Canberra* was able to weigh

The Wessex helicopter of the Queen's Flight, which was piloted by HRH The Prince of Wales, on *Canberra's* midships flight deck.
(Neil McCart)

anchor and leave San Carlos Water. In the early hours of the following morning she rendezvoused with HMS *Hermes* some 138 miles east by north of Stanley. For the next 11 days the *Canberra* remained at sea between 150 and 250 miles east of Stanley, whilst the decisive battles were fought ashore. Although there were serious setbacks, such as the bombing of the landing ships *Sir Galahad* and *Sir Tristram*, the final outcome of the campaign was assured and it was clear that the *Canberra*, as the largest troop transport in the task force, would remain in the area until the final ceasefire was declared. However, despite the optimistic signs, there could be no relaxation of her defences for the Argentine Air Force, even after sustaining heavy losses, remained a potent threat.

The end of the Falklands Campaign came suddenly, with the loss of Wireless Ridge which enabled the British forces to dominate all the open ground west of Stanley, and at 11.22am on Monday 14 June a ceasefire was ordered. That afternoon, whilst steaming in heavy seas some 165 miles east of Stanley, the *Canberra* was ordered to proceed with all haste to San Carlos Water in order to embark prisoners of war. The next stage of the *Canberra's* government service was about to begin. Despite the fact

that there were severe gales blowing, the liner managed to make the passage back to the sheltered waters of Falkland Sound at 24 knots and at just after 1.30pm the following day she anchored once again in San Carlos Water. By this time weather conditions on and around the islands were deteriorating and Major General Jeremy Moore had the problem of finding rations and shelter not only for his own forces, which numbered about 5,000, but also for approximately 10,000 Argentine prisoners of war who would have to be repatriated as quickly as possible. Soon after *Canberra* anchored the first LCU containing men of the Welsh Guards was alongside and 100 POW guards were embarked. They were followed by three more LCUs carrying the Argentine POWs themselves who were allocated cabins on B Deck and below, with the accommodation on A Deck being used by crew members and the embarked service personnel. The POWs were embarked in batches of 200 and taken to the Meridian Room where they were searched and relieved of any weapons and ammunition, and given P&O Cruises luggage labels bearing their deck and cabin number to tie onto their clothing before being escorted to their quarters. Guards were posted in alleyways and on staircases, and it

Surrounded by small boats, the *Canberra* passes Southampton's Town Quay and Royal Pier as the tugs prepare to manoeuvre her alongside in the Western Docks. *(P&O)*

took until the early hours of Wednesday 16 June before all the 1,121 POWs had been dealt with. At 8.15am that morning the *Canberra* left San Carlos Water bound for Port William, the harbour for Stanley, where she was to embark more POWs. Later that afternoon, and all through the night, tenders ferried the Argentine soldiers, most of whom were conscripts relieved to be going home, out to the *Canberra* and by the morning of 17 June there were 4,167 POWs on board.

On Friday 18 June, with diplomatic agreement having been reached, the *Canberra* was able to weigh anchor and set course for Puerto Madryn, a port in the Golfo Nuevo, in the southern province of Chubat. During the 28 hours or so of the voyage home the prisoners had no cause for complaint and one Argentine Army private told later how he and eight of his colleagues were allocated a cabin with a double bed and a single bunk but, as he recounted, '...the floors were nicely carpeted, and we all slept on the floor so that there wouldn't be any arguments about who had the beds.' The same prisoner told how, '...they did treat us well in the *Canberra*. The food was good, and at lunch and dinner we were given two cigarettes each and then allowed

out on the deck for ten minutes, because we were not allowed to smoke in the cabins.' Some of the conscripts had only been in the army for a matter of weeks prior to the Argentine invasion of the Falkland Islands and they told their guards that initially they had thought they were fighting a border war with Chile. According to some members of the *Canberra's* crew, the POWs were generally far less trouble than the average shipload of paying passengers who sailed in the ship for one of her cruises.

At just after 10am on Saturday 19 June, the *Canberra* entered Argentine territorial waters and soon afterwards she was being escorted by the Argentine Navy destroyer *Santissima Trinidad* which, ironically, was a British designed Type 42 warship which had been built under licence at Rio Santiago. By 1.30pm that afternoon the P&O liner was secured, starboard side to, at the private wharf of an aluminium company at Puerto Madryn, which was only a few miles from where the Argentine Marines had practised their landings in preparation for the original invasion of the Falkland Islands. The jetty was a long structure which meant that the *Canberra* was actually berthed about three quarters of a mile from the shoreline.

As the tugs nudge the *Canberra* into her berth the small craft cluster round her and helicopters fly overhead in salute to the 'Great White Whale'.
(Ambrose Greenway)

Parked on the jetty were rows of military trucks and at the bottom of the gangway there were a number of Argentine service officers who were waiting to receive the POWs. Once formalities had been completed the disembarkation could go ahead and it took almost three hours. First ashore were all the wounded who, together with the first hundred or so fit men, received a welcome from the reception committee. However, the majority who followed received no welcome and one prisoner recalls going ashore from the *Canberra*: 'There was no one to meet us. We were put into lorries, and on the drive from the port to the town a lot of people lined the road and were throwing biscuits and other gifts to us.' Some POWs wanted to express genuine thanks to *Canberra's* ship's company and when their cabins were being cleaned and checked, messages of gratitude were found posted on bulkheads. At 5.40pm, with the disembarkation and all the formalities having been completed, the *Canberra* slipped from her berth and set course for Stanley where she was to embark more prisoners for repatriation. She anchored at Port William late in the evening of Sunday 20 June and next day it was learned that she would not, after all, make another voyage to Puerto Madryn but would, instead, embark men of 40 and 42 Commando Royal Marines and return home to Southampton. It was very welcome news.

Over the next two days 42 Commando embarked at Port William and then at 9.50pm on 23 June *Canberra* weighed anchor and set course for San Carlos Water once again where 40 Commando were embarked on the following day. Once this had been completed the *Canberra* returned to Port William in order to collect the Brigade Headquarters, after which she sailed at 5.22pm on Friday 25 June and headed out to sea, into strong winds and driving rain, but no one minded for the ship was bound for Southampton and home.

The voyage north was far more relaxed than the passage south had been and the main worries appeared to revolve around the question of whether the supplies of ice cream and beer would last. As the *Canberra* steamed north and the weather improved, the midships flight deck and all other open spaces became covered with sun worshippers and the Royal Marines Band entertained everyone on a daily basis. On Saturday 3 July the *Canberra* arrived off Ascension Island once again, and during the few hours she spent at the island stores were embarked, including beer, and a few passengers joined for the voyage to Southampton. Among these was the general manager of P&O Cruises who was on board to make advance preparations for the ship's reconversion for cruising, and also a group of singers and entertainers who proved very popular with the troops. Once under way again the liner overtook the P&O ferry MV *Elk* during the afternoon, and on the following day she passed HM ships *Brilliant*, *Rhyl*, *Diomede* and *Danae*, which were also steaming north for home.

By 7am on Saturday 10 July the *Canberra* was some 71 miles south-west of Land's End as she continued her passage home in calm and sunny weather. At 5pm, when the liner was off The Lizard, the P&O chairman Lord Inchcape, together with press representatives, flew on board for the final leg of his ship's long voyage. Some idea of the welcome which awaited them in Southampton was indicated by the number of small boats coming out from every port on the south coast to wave and cheer, and each was acknowledged by the deep boom of the liner's siren. That evening all the crew members and embarked troops were entertained by the Royal Marines Band as they gave their final performance, and in the words of Lt-Cdr John Muxworthy RN, 'Two thousand voices acclaimed the band; two thousand cheered them to the echo. For all of us the band personified what we had done, where we had been and what we had achieved.'

At 6.30am on Sunday 11 July, the *Canberra* was off St Catherine's Point on the Isle of Wight and an hour and a half later she passed the Nab Tower where, as always, the pilot embarked. That morning the troops had been awoken by the harsh sounds of a bugler playing 'Reveille', which was then followed by the gentler tones of Junior Assistant Purser Lois Wheeler making a morning broadcast that all cruising passengers would immediately recognize: 'Good morning ladies and gentlemen. It promises to be a fine day, with every prospect of a warm welcome when we dock. Now if you would care to make your way to the dining halls you will find an early breakfast awaits you. We hope you have enjoyed your cruise and that we might have the pleasure of your company again. Good morning.'

At 9am, as the *Canberra* steamed slowly into the Solent which was bathed in glorious sunshine, HRH The Prince of Wales landed on the midships flight deck in his distinctive red Wessex helicopter of the Queen's Flight, and the liner was surrounded by hundreds of small craft of every description, including canoes paddled by youngsters. It was a far cry from the day, just three months previously, when the *Canberra* had sailed south, for although there had been emotion that day it had been tinged with apprehension. This time all traces of 'British reserve' had been set aside as a real carnival atmosphere gripped the Solent and the city of Southampton. By this time *Canberra* was known to the whole nation as 'The Great White Whale', and although she looked more like a rusty old steamer than a smart passenger liner she was the pride of the British Isles and as she appeared through the mist hundreds of thousands of people lining the shores, and manning the small boats, roared with delight as she moved slowly up Southampton Water. The massive flotilla of small craft, most of them bedecked with bunting and messages of welcome, surrounded her whilst on board the Royal Marines packed every available vantage point on the starboard side, with some of the more enterprising of them

The climax of the *Canberra's* triumphant return to Southampton. Hundreds of balloons fly aloft as the liner is nudged into her berth. *(The News, Portsmouth)*

even climbing into the lifeboats. The men had draped their own messages over the ship's side, many of them reflecting the humour of British servicemen.

As the enormous procession of boats, yachts and ferries, including the cross-Channel ferry *Dragon*, made its way towards the *Canberra's* berth in the Western Docks, it was met by the port's fireboats which added their cascades of water to the scene of gaily coloured flags and bunting. Every few minutes the *Canberra's* deep siren boomed its reply to the shouts, cheers and whistles of all those present, whether on the water or ashore. An overwhelming tide of emotion followed the 'White Whale' as she steamed slowly but proudly into her home port.

As she drew level with the Eastern Docks a squadron of Lynx helicopters trailing coloured smoke roared overhead and the ship came to a stop, as if she was unable to move for the masses of small boats which were gathered around her. She had, in fact, slowed down to allow the Prince of Wales and other VIPs to depart in his Wessex helicopter. The Prince had met about 60 crew members and 300 Royal Marines in a reception held in the Meridian Room but, being determined not to steal the limelight of the welcome which he felt should be enjoyed by those who had served in the South Atlantic, he left before the ship docked alongside 106 berth.

At her berth the P&O shore staff had hung out dozens of welcoming banners and messages to decorate the quayside, and as the *Canberra's* huge bulk was edged into the berth, the whole emotional welcome reached its climax. The Royal Marines Band struck up 'Land of Hope and Glory' with the full choral accompaniment of the Marines on board and the enormous crowds in the Western Docks. Without a doubt, the sight of this great liner so vulnerable and at the mercy of the Argentine Air Force, had won the hearts of the nation. The statistics of the *Canberra's* 94 days at sea with the task force make impressive reading. She steamed 25,245 nautical miles, and did not suffer a single mechanical failure of any major machinery. Her evaporators produced 39,522 tons of fresh water; the galley served 650,000 meals with the bakery producing over one million bread rolls. It can be proudly claimed that the *Canberra* landed most of the ground forces who went into action on the Falkland Islands and, as well as operating as a troop transport, she acted as a hospital ship and prisoner transport, and provided much needed rest and recreation for hard-pressed task force units.

The *Canberra* had been the heroine of 'Operation Corporate', the campaign to recapture the Falkland Islands, but now the time had come to restore her to pristine condition for her true role - that of a leisurely cruise ship.

The aftermath - hundreds of soiled pillows are stacked into the Cricketers' Tavern ready to be taken ashore. *(P&O)*

Chapter Eleven

The Return To Trade

The *Canberra's* triumphant return to Southampton on 11 July 1982 after her gruelling three-month Falkland 'cruise' was a relief for the P&O management for, although the charter rates paid by the Government ensured that the company suffered no financial loss, the fact that Russian and Ukranian cruise ships were still cruising from UK ports was a serious threat to P&O's established market. Although *Canberra* had suffered no structural damage, the superstructure amidships and forward had to be totally refitted and the internal furnishings had been subjected to a great deal of wear and tear. The vessel went into Southampton's King George V Dry Dock on 9 August and she emerged three weeks later. The biggest single factor in the refit was of course the restoration of her observation deck forward and the midships pool, not to mention the vast quantities of white paint which were needed to restore her hull and superstructure. Inside the ship most of the work involved refitting, renewing and refurbishing carpets, soft furnishings and internal decoration.

During the refit P&O made some alterations to the accommodation, which included air-conditioning in the Stadium and the installation of a new bar on the starboard side of the Island Room. The reason given for the additional air-conditioning was the fact that she was to spend the UK winter cruising from Sydney at the height of

Still wearing her 'battle scars', the *Canberra* lies alongside 106 berth before being towed to the dry dock for the start of her post-Falklands refit.

(Neil McCart)

the Australian summer but, in the event, the *Canberra's* cruising role based on Sydney proved to be very limited. In the Crow's Nest the forest of scaffolding which had supported the weight of the forward flight deck was removed, together with the yards of sacking which had been wound round the securing bolts and the heavy wooden blocks which had shored up the metal poles. The deep pile carpets from the room, which had been put into storage, were laid down again. Many of the officers who had used the bar will always remember the 'hanging habit' as it became known - as they reached up and grabbed an overhead pole while enjoying a pint of beer. There was even one - there always is - who went one better and perfected the party trick of hanging upside down from the scaffolding. In addition to all the routine refurbishment on board, a Southampton piano tuner had to be brought in to restore and retune all the *Canberra's* pianos which had been adversely affected by the extra vibration caused by the helicopters landing and taking off.

Initially it was thought that the liner would make a shakedown cruise before resuming her normal service on 11 September 1982, having missed 12 cruises. However, in the event that was not to be and she sailed on schedule for a 14-day voyage to Gibraltar, Corfu, Loutraki, Palma and Vigo. Had it not been for the campaign in the South Atlantic it would have been her thirteenth cruise and there were now only three left before the end of her UK season. When she left Southampton on 11 September on the first of these cruises, the port and city gave her a warm send-off. Once again the fireboats came out to greet her and large crowds gathered, and as the *Canberra* pulled away from her berth it was fitting that she was saluted by the Atlantic survey vessel *John Biscoe* which was berthed nearby. This time she was escorted down the Solent by the training ship *Malcolm Miller* as well as a number of small craft.

The *Canberra* completed her final three cruises of the 1982 season on Friday 22 October, when she arrived in Southampton from an Atlantic Islands cruise to Madeira, Las Palmas and Tenerife, returning by way of Gibraltar and Lisbon. She was immediately taken over once again by Vospers for a further 18-day refit. Although she was berthed in the port's dry dock it was because of the excellent cranage facilities and there was no need to drain the dock. The underwater hull, including her propellers, had been thoroughly inspected during her post-Falklands refit and the liner's mechanical reliability had already proved itself during the second of her three 1982 cruises when, following a ten-hour delay at Palma because of high winds, she had steamed home to Southampton at 25 knots and had arrived early on the morning of Saturday 9 October, right on schedule.

During the refit there was a minor fire on board which delayed her sailing by three days, and she finally left Southampton for her voyage to Sydney on Friday 12

November. During the passage via Panama and San Francisco she was able to make up time and she arrived in Sydney only a day late, just three days before Christmas. On the quayside at the Overseas Passenger Terminal to meet *Canberra* was her sponsor Dame Pattie Menzies, who had lunch on board with Captain Scott-Masson. She was obviously still very interested in 'her' ship and remarked, 'I was terribly worried about *Canberra* while she was in the South Atlantic. But the captain was good enough to send me a cable as the ship left the Falklands to say she had come through unscathed.'

The *Canberra's* 1983 cruising season from Southampton began on 15 April with bookings for her programme of 13 cruises significantly up on the previous year, which was partly attributed to the 'Falklands Factor'. For the first time ever all her berths were fully booked, which was achieved by the immense publicity the ship had attracted through her trooping activities with the task force, and also by the reallocation of bookings that had been cancelled after her requisition in April 1982, for many of the *Canberra's* passengers had remained intensely loyal to the ship. On Friday 20 May 1983 the Royal Marines bandsmen who had sailed for the Falkland Islands just over a year earlier were back on board, but this time for a cruise to the Atlantic Islands. The 44-strong band, under their musical director Captain John Ware RM, provided a dance band, a 20-piece salon orchestra, a trad jazz band and a string quartet. The musicians gave two military concerts and on Tuesday 31 May, whilst the ship was alongside at Vigo, they performed their famous ceremony of Beating Retreat. The first day of the cruise, at sea between Southampton and Lisbon, was also the first anniversary of the landings at San Carlos, and this was commemorated with a special programme devised by Captain Ware.

On Saturday 3 September that year, during a 16-night Mediterranean cruise, the *Canberra* made her first extended, 32-hour, visit to Port Said in Egypt as part of her cruise programme. Of course the ships of the P&O and, indeed, the *Canberra* herself, were no strangers to the port, but these calls had always been of just a few hours duration to await the start of a southbound convoy or at the end of a northbound transit of the Suez Canal. This time it was as a visit to the port in its own right and passengers were able to make a trip to the Pyramids or the Nile, or even take the short drive down the west bank of the Suez Canal to the town of Ismailia. The occasion was marked by a visit from the Governor of Port Said, Mr Sayed Sarham, who attended a reception on board and presented Captain Bob Ellingham with a plaque bearing the badge of Port Said.

On 23 October 1983, at the end of her cruise season, the *Canberra* was taken over by Southampton's Vosper Thorneycroft shipyard to undergo a 17-day overhaul at a cost of £1,600,000. Only a few weeks previously the contract to refit the *QE2* had gone to a German shipyard,

The Cricketers' Tavern, as it looked in the final years of the *Canberra's* career, refurbished and as magnificent as it was in 1961.　　　*(Peter Knego)*

Canberra's Island Room at the after end of the Games Deck as the room looked when the ship ended her service in 1997.　　　*(Peter Knego)*

A magnificent aerial view of the *Canberra* as she lies high and dry in Southampton's King George V Graving Dock undergoing her refit. The dockside crane is removing the large steel plates over the Bonito Pool which formed the midships flight deck, and the guard rails and windscreens have already been replaced.

(Southern Newspapers Ltd)

Restored to her original pristine condition, the *Canberra* is back alongside Southampton's 106 berth, and ready to start cruising once again. *(Neil McCart)*

for lunch. In the hot sunshine of Sydney the atmosphere was very different from the South Atlantic, but the *Canberra's* surgeon, Dr Peter Maynard, was able to renew his acquaintance with the carrier's surgeon, Commander Richard Moody RN. The *Canberra's* sailing team even challenged the Australian Navy to compete in a dinghy sailing race, but unfortunately, they had to concede defeat.

The *Canberra's* return to Southampton on Wednesday 11 April 1984 was again made via Panama, with calls at Port Everglades and New York before the eastbound Atlantic crossing by way of Madeira. In early June, during a two-day stopover in Southampton, the *Canberra's* profile was altered slightly with the addition of a 'Mascot 2000' satellite communications terminal, which increased the ship's worldwide and all-weather voice and telex coverage. Initially the UK cruising sesason went well, but in July that year strikes by some of Southampton's dock workers closed the port. The closure affected both the *Canberra* and the *QE2* and upon her return from the Mediterranean on 15 July 1984, the *Canberra* was diverted to Cherbourg and both the incoming and departing passengers were flown to and from Hurn Airport, Bournemouth. This massive airlift of over 3,000 passengers was an extremely expensive operation and it was particularly inconvenient with P&O moving its cruising department from London to Southampton at the same time. The airlift of passengers had to be repeated on Friday 7 September.

That summer the ship played a part in the filming of a TV series 'Tenko', the story of Far Eastern prisoners of war. *Canberra* took the role of her predecessor of the 1930s, SS *Ranchi*, which had repatriated civilian internees from Singapore back home to Britain in September 1945. Over 100 film extras, all clad in 1940s tropical outfits, transformed part of 106 berth to resemble Singapore's Keppel Harbour and the *Canberra* sported an SS *Ranchi* gangway.

The *Canberra's* 1984 UK season ended on Monday 22 October, when she returned from a 16-night cruise to the eastern Mediterranean for her annual overhaul. Nineteen days later, on Saturday 10 November, the vessel left Southampton bound, once again, for the US West Coast and then Sydney where she would carry out her final cruise programme from the Australian port, for it had been decided that the 90-day world cruise would be reinstated.

During 1984 the *Canberra* had consolidated her position as the country's favourite cruise ship, but for one family she is an extra-special ship. The story of young Simon Gill and his family is best told by the ship's Cruise Director, Phil Raymond: 'In 1980 the Gill family sailed on their first cruising holiday in *Canberra*. They had a fabulous time and went home full of happy memories and their young son, Simon, was so overwhelmed by it all that he wanted to work on board when he was old enough. His enthusiasm and his happy memories of the *Canberra* were to play a very important part in his life.

but by guaranteeing the quality of the work and giving a firm date for completion, the British company were able to secure this very valuable work on the *Canberra*. However, no sooner had the refit started than there was the threat of a strike at the yard and the completion date could no longer be guaranteed, which led to the proposed dry docking being cancelled. Although the internal refurbishment work could be carried out whilst the *Canberra* was alongside 106 berth, the major part of the contract entailed the dry docking. The resultant publicity did little to help the reputation of British shipbuilders, but in the event *Canberra* was able to leave Southampton as scheduled during the afternoon of Thursday 10 November bound for Panama, the West Coast of the USA and Sydney. With the ship almost fully booked for her positioning voyage and also well booked for a Christmas cruise from Sydney, P&O could not take any chances on the ship not being ready for sea. While in Sydney she met HMS *Invincible* which was on a goodwill visit to the port, and to commemorate their time together in the South Atlantic the *Invincible's* wardroom invited the *Canberra's* officers on board

Dressed overall the *Canberra* arrives at Sydney during her final world cruise in early 1997. It was to be her last visit to the port.
(Reid - Fairfax Photo Library)

In the early morning sunshine at 7.30am on 14 March 1997 the *Canberra* made her final call at San Francisco. In the background is the infamous Alcatraz Island and Prison.
(Marvin Jensen)

A little bit of black smoke, but at last the *Canberra* is ready to embark her usual paying passengers once again. *(Neil McCart)*

In July 1983, tragedy struck when he and his sister were on their way to catch the school bus and he was hit by a car travelling at 48mph. He received multiple injuries, including brain damage, and he was taken to hospital in a coma. He remained unconscious for some time but, when he regained consciousness, he showed no sign of recognition of anything or anyone. When he was taken home from hospital it was accepted that he would probably never be able to communicate again. One evening, on television, the *Canberra's* Falklands refit was being featured. Miraculously Simon sat up, pointed at the screen and, in his own way, made noises of recognition at seeing the ship. The next day his father booked a holiday on the *Canberra* and when

Simon embarked he was in a wheelchair. We made friends with him and I found that, with a little time, I could understand everything he said and that there was an intelligent lad in there desperately trying to get out. After two weeks he was taking occasional walks, a couple of steps at a time. On the last day as I stood on the quayside at Southampton saying farewell to passengers, I was surprised to see the boy's father come down the gangway alone with the wheelchair under his arm. "Where's Simon?" I asked. "Here's one passenger who insists on walking off on his own," he replied smiling as Simon slowly but surely stepped ashore unaided. Every heart on board went out to brave little Simon, his sister Victoria and his parents. *Canberra* is proud to have played yet another important role, that of giving hope back to a brave little boy whose family were on the verge of losing hope. *Canberra* is "special".'

On her arrival back from Australia in March 1985, the *Canberra* underwent an overhaul at the German shipyard of Lloyd Werft at Bremerhaven. Vospers Shiprepairers of Southampton were invited to tender for the work, but at the time they were involved in a lingering process of privatization and had failed to win a number of contracts. In June 1985 *Canberra* was delayed just as she was about to depart on a Fjords cruise, when members of the National Union of Seamen went on strike in protest against plans to cut wages and make stewards more reliant on tips from passengers. On 10 July the AGM of the Missions to Seamen was held on board, and the event was attended by the President of the Mission, Princess Anne, who arrived at the docks by helicopter. After being received on board by the managing director of P&O Cruises there was a reception, followed by lunch in the Pacific Restaurant hosted by Captain David Hannah.

In May 1986, the ex-Orient liner, *Oriana*, which had entered service only seven months before the *Canberra* and which had operated as both a passenger liner and a cruise ship, was withdrawn from service. This left the *Canberra* as the last of the company's fast mail steamers and she now took the title of 'Cock of the Fleet' which, by tradition, was given to the fastest ship in the P&O fleet. The *Oriana* had taken the title on 26 May 1963 whilst on passage from

Saluted by a Southampton firefloat, the *Canberra* leaves for her first post-Falklands cruise. (*Neil McCart*)

Suez to Aden, when she had made a record noon to noon day's run of 701 nautical miles at an average speed of 29.21 knots. However, in setting the record she had used 451 tons of furnace fuel oil, which would not be acceptable in these days of conservation. Upon the *Oriana's* withdrawal the large sheet brass silhouette of a cockerel, which had been carried above the old Orient liner's navigation bridge, was transferred to the *Canberra**.

In late 1985 P&O Cruises announced that, as part of her 1986 summer cruise programme, *Canberra* would make ten 'special interest' cruises which offered lectures and instruction by leading experts in their fields. These were to become very popular and included well-known personalities such as the astronomer, Patrick Moore. Some of the other themes featured were gardening, ornithology, food and wine, golf and classical music. However, during the summer cruise season it was none of these which gained the most publicity, but a very unwelcome mystery illness which plagued passengers on eight cruises between early May and mid-August, breaking out first during a voyage to the eastern Mediterranean. Eventually the virus was identified and by the end of September the ship was free of the sickness, but it had ensured that the *Canberra* received a great deal of adverse publicity.

No sooner had the problem of the viral infection dropped out of the news than the *Canberra* hit the headlines once again, this time when it was announced that the vessel's £3 million annual refit was to be carried out at the Lloyd Werft shipyard at Bremerhaven, and not in Southampton. During the refit, which actually took place

between 30 November and 18 December 1986, the opportunity was taken to completely redesign the Peacock Room; it was renamed Neptunes and transformed into an attractive nightclub. The William Fawcett Room was also totally refurbished and renamed the Ocean Room, a name which had originally been intended for the room in 1960. New furnishings and lighting were fitted in the Pacific Restaurant while the Atlantic Restaurant was redesigned and refurbished throughout. The Meridian Room was remodelled and refurbished, and various points around the ship such as the Promenade Shop and Bonito Club and various foyers were all given a new look. A permanent buffet was installed in the Island Room and improvements to the passenger accommodation included the construction of 20 new staterooms on A deck in place of a number of court cabins. New carpets were fitted along all the main companionways on A, B, Promenade and C Decks, and this added touch of luxury had the effect of transforming and modernizing *Canberra's* passenger accommodation. The tasteful pastel shades and potted plants in the public rooms created a similar atmosphere to that found in the *Royal Princess*, which was then P&O's most modern cruise ship and which had been built for Princess Cruises. The whole of G Deck, which had once accommodated 96 tourist class passengers in four-berth cabins, was set aside for the professional theatre players on board, and the Stadium Theatre itself was fitted with permanent tiered seating for perfect views of the stage during gala shows and variety performances.

A number of important improvements were also

* The cockerel was finally handed over to the company's latest *Oriana* in the very last days of the *Canberra's* service.

planned for the daily cruise routine of the ship such as a much improved ship's newspaper, longer opening hours for the night nursery, additional writing facilities in public rooms and a gymnasium on the starboard side of the Games Deck which had once housed the table tennis room. The improvements also included the upgrading of menus, changes to the wine list and restyling of officers' uniforms. Modifications were also made to itineraries, with most UK cruises for the 1987 season starting, whenever possible, on Saturdays and with longer stopovers in ports of call to allow passengers more time ashore. A few new ports were added to the ship's itinerary and dates were arranged so that seven-day fly-cruises could be made.

One crew member, the Assistant Head Waiter, recalled the transformation at the Lloyd Werft shipyard: 'When I joined the *Canberra* at Bremerhaven after her refit, along with 200 other crew members two days before we sailed for Southampton from the dry dock, it didn't seem possible that she would sail on 19 December for the Christmas Cruise. Everywhere there were cables, acetylene cutters and welders, painters, joiners, carpet layers and wallpaperers. Public rooms had chairs and tables piled ceiling high and everything was covered with dust and wood chippings. But sail she did - and on time too.'

This 'new look' *Canberra* made her first post-refit cruise from Southampton on 19 December 1986, on a Christmas and New Year voyage to the west African ports of Freetown and Dakar, and the Atlantic Isles and, according to the Assistant Head Waiter, 'The whole cruise was a wonderful success with a packed ship. I knew a few of the passengers who remembered *Canberra* as she was and they had nothing but praise for the new look. One of the highlights of the cruise was on New Year's Eve. After leaving our berth in Madeira we steamed up and down the coast and at midnight a magnificent New Year firework display was put on by the community of Madeira. On the stroke of midnight all the ships in harbour, and outside, blew their sirens, whistles and hooters, heralding in the New Year. On shore more fireworks were set off along the mountain range surrounding Funchal and in the town itself.' Following this cruise, on Tuesday 6 January 1987, she left Southampton for her 34,000-mile world cruise during which she would call at 23 ports from Los Angeles to Sydney and Hong Kong.

The *Canberra's* route took her by way of the Panama Canal into the Pacific Ocean where she was scheduled to call at Acapulco and Los Angeles, but whilst she was off the Mexican Pacific coast she was involved in the highly publicized rescue of a family of five who were adrift in a small inflatable dinghy. Mr Joshua Jones, a computer engineer from Berkshire, had left his comfortable lifestyle in October 1982, and with his wife and three children had set off in his 35-ft ketch, *Dorothy Anne*, to sail round the world. Four years later, in November 1986, they had left

Australia on the homeward leg of their long voyage and in late January 1987 they were off the coast of Mexico. There they encountered bad weather and tried to hug the coast as they made their way towards the Bay of Panama and Balboa. Their real drama started at 8.30pm on Friday 23 January 1987, when two enormous waves hit the *Dorothy Anne*, snapped her tiller and caused her to ship water faster than her pumps could discharge it. It was clear that the ketch was sinking fast and the Joneses started preparing to abandon ship. After Mr Jones had cut the life dinghy free and pushed it into the stormy sea, the family, who had roped themselves together, found themselves swimming in the sea on a very stormy and dark night, but they managed to get aboard the 7-ft round dinghy. That night, as they rode out the storm, the dinghy was was actually turned upside down but luck, and the craft's canopy, helped save them as they prepared for a very long wait with only limited rations. Fortunately, the following day they were spotted by a Korean freighter, *Rainier*, which saw one of their emergency flares but, with a heavy sea still running, she was unable to rescue them herself and she put out a rescue alert. Fortunately, the *Canberra*, commanded by Captain David Hannah, was approaching Acapulco and being only 12 miles away from the dinghy she was soon on the scene. With a 15-ft swell running, a rescue by boat would have been dangerous and Captain Hannah decided to attempt to bring the *Canberra* alongside the raft from windward which would give it a lee and allow the cruise ship to drift onto the raft. He ordered the engines to 'manoeuvring revolutions' and both accident boats to be turned out, in case they were needed. Scrambling ladders were rigged and a very slow approach was made in order to assess drift, with the raft slightly off the port bow.

So good was Captain Hannah's seamanship that the *Canberra's* first approach was successful and the great white liner drifted so gently on to the dinghy that the occupants were able to grasp a boat rope which had been lowered. Then Able Seaman Tim Buckler climbed down to the bottom of a pilot ladder and helped the Jones family into the safety of the *Canberra*. They were taken to the ship's hospital where they were found to be none the worse for their terrifying ordeal and they were allocated two empty cabins until the ship reached Los Angeles. From there they flew on to Heathrow where they arrived on 30 January, a week after the loss of their ketch and some months ahead of their schedule. Two months later, when the *Canberra* returned to Southampton at the end of her world cruise, the Jones family again went aboard - up the gangway in the normal manner - to greet the ship and to present a family photograph with their ill-fated ketch *Dorothy Anne* to the captain.

On Saturday 19 September 1987, whilst at Southampton between cruises, the *Canberra* played host to an anniversary dinner held to celebrate the ship's

On Tuesday 30 September 1997 the *Canberra* made a triumphant final arrival at Southampton, when she was escorted by HMS *Cornwall*, firefloats and hundreds of small boats. In this view the crowds fill Mayflower Park to say their farewells to an old friend.
(Ian Spashett)

Thousands of balloons are released by passengers as the *Canberra* approaches her berth in Southampton Docks for the last time. This photograph was taken from the frigate HMS *Cornwall*.
(Mark Histed)

On the afternoon of 10 November 1984 the *Canberra* prepares to depart for her world cruise via Panama, whilst aft of her lies the *Royal Princess* preparing for her maiden voyage nine days later.

(R. Bruce Grice)

commissioning for the Falklands campaign, as well as P&O's 150th anniversary. The principal guest was Princess Anne who presided over a gathering of service personnel, including Admiral of the Fleet Sir Henry Leach, as well as merchant seamen and the company's shore-based staff who also played a vital role during the campaign. After the dinner the 300 guests watched the ceremony of Beating Retreat by the band of the Royal Marines. The occasion had originally been scheduled for March that year but had been postponed following the disaster which befell the P&O controlled ferry, *Herald of Free Enterprise*.

By the end of the 1980s the *Canberra* was, without a doubt, Britain's favourite cruise ship. With her appetizing food, the familiar currency and her well-trained officers, the atmosphere she exuded was uniquely and reassuringly British, no matter where she was in the world. It was just what her passengers wanted.

A very popular port for the *Canberra's* summer cruising season was Malta. Here she is seen off the breakwater of Grand Harbour as the tugs manoeuvre her past Valletta's ancient fortifications...

...to her berth in Bighi Bay, where once the Royal Navy's Mediterranean Fleet dominated the scene. In the background is the imposing building of the old Bighi Naval Hospital.

(Michael Cassar)

Chapter Twelve

The Final Decade

By the end of the 1980s the *Canberra* had established her position as Britain's premier cruise ship, but she was almost 30 years old and there were continual rumours about her replacement. More and more she was being dogged by machinery defects, but these were really only minor problems and they were far outweighed by the fact that her accommodation was in good condition, and that she was still very popular with the public. In June 1989, on an 18-night voyage to the Mediterranean, during which she called at Istanbul and the Black Sea port of Varna, Bulgaria, she suffered problems in one of her main propulsion motors which put her behind schedule, and technical experts were flown out to Malaga to work on the engine whilst the ship was en route to Southampton. Passengers on the cruise enjoyed an extra day at sea, but those who were booked on the next cruise, a nine-night voyage to the Iberian Islands, lost a day of their holiday.

At the end of that year, during *Canberra's* 17-night Christmas Cruise, she suffered a complete power failure on board, just hours after leaving Southampton on the evening of Wednesday 20 December. Although this particular problem was overcome, bad weather and mechanical faults continued to cause difficulties and she failed to reach Freetown in Sierra Leone. Instead she made an unscheduled stop at the Cape Verde Islands, where she had to anchor offshore and on her return to Southampton the company had to discuss compensation for her passengers. It was clear that the *Canberra* was in the final phase of her long career.

Despite her mechanical problems, as the last decade of the century opened the *Canberra* was still as popular as ever with holidaymakers, and when she left on her world cruise on the evening of Monday 8 January 1990 she was well booked. The voyage took her across the Atlantic Ocean by way of Madeira and Bermuda, before calling at Fort

During the 1980s and early 1990s the *Canberra's* public rooms were extensively refurnished and modernized. This view shows the refurbished Atlantic Restaurant. Compare this view with that in Chapter Three.　　　*(Neil McCart)*

The Meridian Room without its spindly 1960s furniture, but with the much more comfortable and luxurious sofas demanded by the passengers in the late 20th century. *(Neil McCart)*

Lauderdale, Montego Bay and Bonaire as she made her way to Panama and the US West Coast. From San Francisco she steamed to Honolulu, Fiji and on to Auckland and Sydney. She left Australia on Thursday 22 February and steamed north to Honiara, Rabaul and the Taiwanese port of Keelung before steaming south-west to Hong Kong, Pattaya in Thailand, and Singapore. Her voyage home from South-East Asia was reminiscent of an earlier era when P&O's 'China Boats' plied the trade routes of the east for, after calling at Port Kelang (formerly Port Swettenham), she steamed to Bombay and on into the Red Sea, finally calling at Piraeus and Naples before arriving in Southampton on the morning of Monday 9 April 1990.

It was in August 1991, whilst the *Canberra* was returning home from a two-week cruise to the Adriatic, that the first indications came from P&O that they were actively considering the ship's future. On 21 August they announced that they were proposing to raise £604 million by way of a rights issue of new deferred stock. The annoucement went on to outline the fact that the most capital-intensive part of the P&O Group's business was shipping, and that as the cruise division faced well-

equipped foreign fleets it was important that the necessary capital was available to maintain the quality of P&O's vessels. Referring specifically to the cruising fleet the following statement was made: 'P&O has recently taken delivery of *Regal Princess*, the third of three new cruise ships. Active consideration is being given to the construction, over the next few years, of a further Princess cruise ship and the replacement of *Canberra*, each at a cost of some £200 million.'

At the start of her 1991 cruise season the *Canberra* had been joined by the *Sea Princess*, formerly the Swedish Amerika liner *Kungsholm*, and the two vessels would cruise in tandem for the remaining years of the *Canberra's* career. During the cruising season, with the Soviet Union about to disintegrate, the *Canberra* was able to make a voyage into the Black Sea to the ports of Odessa and Yalta. At the end of the season, and for the first time for nine years, the *Canberra* underwent her annual overhaul at Southampton. The 11-day refit was carried out by A&P Southampton and as well as refurbishing the passenger accommodation, they carried out tank surveys, maintenance on the structural steelwork and mechanical work in the ship's

The Bonito Club, 1990s style.   (Neil McCart)

machinery. Normally the liner would not have been dry docked, but with the *Sea Princess* using 106 berth an alternative was needed for the *Canberra* and the King George V Graving Dock was the ideal option. At the end of her refit, in mid-December, the *Canberra* made her Christmas and New Year cruise to Dakar and the Atlantic Islands, before leaving the UK on the evening of Saturday 4 January 1992 for her world voyage which included Picton on New Zealand's south island, Guam in the Mariana Islands, Kobe and Kagoshima in Japan, Port Louis in Mauritius and the South African ports of Durban and Cape Town. This change of route on the homeward leg was as a result of the 1991 Gulf War which meant that ships could not make the traditional passage via the Suez Canal.

In January 1992 P&O placed an order for a new, 67,000-ton cruise ship from the Meyer Werft shipyard at Papenburg, Germany. She was the first ever cruise ship to be custom-built for the British market and the scheduled delivery date was April 1995. It was a further reminder of the *Canberra's* advancing years, and the fact that quite clearly she was rapidly approaching the end of her career.

However, her cruising schedule continued as before,

although in 1992 the Yugoslavian port of Dubrovnik, from where passengers had always explored the old cities of Mostar and Kotor, had to be removed from her itinerary as a brutal war ravaged the confederation of the southern Slavic people, Serbs, Slovenes, Croats and Montenegrins, which had come into being in November 1918 following the collapse of the Habsburg Empire. The *Canberra's* cruising season that year ended with her traditional Christmas and New Year cruise to West Africa and the ports of Dakar and Freetown, with the New Year being welcomed in off Funchal, Madeira, where she became a floating grandstand for the huge firework display which the islanders put on for tourists.

On her arrival in Southampton on Monday 4 January 1993 preparations were quickly put in hand for her annual world cruise and on the evening of Wednesday 6 January the *Canberra* left the port bound for Madeira, Charleston, Fort Lauderdale, Montego Bay, Curacao and Panama. Twelve days after leaving her home port, when she was between Charleston and Fort Lauderdale, she suffered mechanical problems which held her up at the latter port for eight days and put her well behind schedule. However,

During the latter part of her career the *Canberra* cruised from Southampton in tandem with the *Victoria*, formerly the Swedish liner *Kungsholm* and P&O's *Sea Princess*. (M. Beckett)

the delay solved a problem for the Police in Sussex who had been trying to trace an infamous woman who was well known on the London vice scene. The woman's car had been found near a famous suicide spot at Beachy Head, and bizarre stories appeared in the British press that she might have been killed or abducted after she had threatened to publish the names of 'clients' at her brothel, said to include Members of Parliament and Peers. In the event she was traced to the *Canberra* and the police search in the UK was called off. The publicity generated in the press overshadowed the vessel's mechanical problems, although it was 25 April before the liner left Fort Lauderdale for Panama. The end of the cruise, like the start, was dominated by the latest news of the ship's notorious passenger, as police officers waited on the quayside at Southampton to interview her.

In the spring of 1993 the official keel-laying ceremony for the new 67,000-ton cruise ship took place in the Meyer Werft shipyard when the first two sections were laid in a dry dock, and it was announced that the new vessel would be named *Oriana*. It was also announced that she would

operate alongside both the *Canberra* and the *Sea Princess* as the company anticipated an unprecedented growth in the numbers of passengers taking cruising holidays. For the *Canberra* the 1993 season followed a familiar pattern and on Thursday 6 January 1994 she left Southampton on her 90-day world voyage by way of Panama.

It was during the world cruise, as the *Canberra* steamed across the Arabian Sea between Bombay and the Jordanian port of Aqaba in the Red Sea, that an emergency call for assistance was received from a liquefied gas carrier, *Hilli*, which was en route from the Persian Gulf to Japan. In fact it was not the *Hilli* which was in trouble, but the Maltese-flagged oil tanker *Stolide* which had loaded 65,000 tons of crude oil for South Korea. She had left port for her destination when, on the morning of Sunday 20 March 1994, she suffered a massive explosion and flash fire which killed 18 of her crew members instantaneously and badly injured at least 11 others. At the time of the explosion the *Stolide* was in the Arabian Sea, some 250 miles off the Omani island of Masira (once an RAF staging post), and the *Hilli* was the first rescue ship to reach the stricken

Beneath the volcanic rocks of Santa Cruz, the *Canberra* arrives at Tenerife during an Atlantic Islands cruise.   *(Mike Lennon)*

tanker. However, of the 19 crew members who were picked up by the gas carrier, two died of their injuries and nine others were suffering from severe burns which the *Hilli's* medical facilities were not equipped to treat and so she immediately put out the urgent request for assistance.

Captain Ian Gibb of the *Canberra* diverted the liner from her scheduled route to rendezvous with the *Hilli* and at the agreed point the *Canberra* sent away two of her lifeboats, along with a medical team, to transfer the five most seriously injured survivors before resuming her westerly course towards the Red Sea. Once back on board the *Canberra* it was realized that two of the injured crewmen, a Filipino seaman and the Greek Second Mate, were suffering 60 per cent and 30 per cent burns respectively and required immediate hospital treatment. In that region the best facilities available were, in fact, at Djibouti, the small French outpost on the north coast of the Somali Republic, and as the *Canberra* steamed through the Gulf of Aden a French military helicopter flew out to the liner to transfer the two men to a hospital ashore. Meanwhile, as the drama unfolded on board the *Canberra*, the *Hilli* disembarked her remaining survivors at Oman,

before continuing her voyage east to Japan. On board the liner, Captain Ian Gibb, on behalf of his crew and the *Canberra's* 1,500 passengers, expressed sadness at the loss of life, but as he said, 'Once again *Canberra* has responded with speed and efficiency, which is a tribute to the ship's company and the vessel itself. We are doing everything at our disposal to ensure the comfort of the survivors.' As the *Canberra* steamed through the Red Sea her passengers and ship's company organized a collection and raised over £5,000 for the injured men and their dependants. For the liner the saga finally ended on Saturday 26 March, when the remaining crew members from the *Stolide* were diembarked at Aqaba.

The *Canberra* arrived back at Southampton on the morning of Thursday 7 April 1994 and two days later her UK cruising season opened with a 25-night voyage which took her across the Atlantic to the USA and the Caribbean. The highlight of the year for the *Canberra* was the 50th Anniversary of the historic D-Day landings on 6 June 1944, when the Allied powers landed on the heavily defended northern French coast. The *Canberra* arrived back in Southampton from a 16-night cruise to Port Said and the Eastern Mediterranean on the morning of Wednesday 1 June and three days later, during the afternoon of Saturday 4 June, she embarked hundreds of D-Day veterans and their families for a short cruise which had been organized by the Royal British Legion. For many of those present the embarkation at Southampton must have evoked memories of the events 50 years before, but the luxury of the P&O cruise ship ensured that they did not have to endure anything like the cramped and spartan conditions of those times. That same day the *Canberra* left her berth to join the assortment of naval and merchant ships which were taking their places at Spithead anchorages in preparation for the review by Her Majesty The Queen and the US President Bill Clinton, which would take place the next day. Amongst the big ships taking part were the giant US Navy aircraft carrier USS *George Washington* and the smaller Royal Navy carrier HMS *Illustrious*, both of them bristling with aircraft and weaponry which would have been unimaginable in 1944. On a more peaceful theme, and flying the red duster, were the *QE2* and *Canberra* and even two vintage vessels which would not have been out of place in the Solent all those years ago, the US Liberty ship *Jeremiah O'Brien* and the Clyde paddle steamer *Waverley*.

Having embarked in the *Canberra* in the rain, it was a great relief to her passengers to find that Sunday 5 June dawned bright and sunny, although windy, as a flotilla of small ships joined the larger vessels at Spithead. One veteran aboard the *Canberra*, a former army sergeant from Yorkshire, perhaps echoed the thoughts of all those present when he remarked, 'I just can't believe it was 50 years ago. It seems like yesterday.'

Meanwhile ashore, on a sunny Southsea Common, the Queen, President Clinton and 11 other foreign leaders attended a drumhead service before driving to Portsmouth Dockyard to embark in the royal yacht *Britannia*. There is no doubt that Britain's heritage of ceremony was ideal and very appropriate as shortly after midday *Britannia*, led by the Trinity House vessel *Patricia*, steamed out of Portsmouth Harbour after a fly-past of wartime military aircraft led by a lumbering 'stringbag' Swordfish biplane. The *Britannia* was accompanied by a flotilla of 19 ships, as well as a free-for-all of literally hundreds of yachts and power boats which, somehow, seemed entirely appropriate and added to the atmosphere of the occasion. The Queen, accompanied by President Clinton and other heads of state, stood on deck as the royal yacht steamed between two files of the ships drawn up for the review. The *Britannia* then led the fleet into the Channel for the voyage to France.

In mid-Channel there was another review while on the *Canberra's* Sun Deck the veterans and their families gathered round the Bonito Pool for a remembrance service. As the *Britannia* steamed by, one ship of each nation cast a wreath into the sea and at the same time a Lancaster bomber flew low over the *Canberra* to drop 850,000 red poppies onto the liner's deck. Many of the veterans considered this to be the most moving event of the commemorations. During the short cruise the *Canberra's* public rooms evoked the world of the 1940s, with the music of Glenn Miller and songs from Vera Lynn and Gracie Fields. It was the era of the foxtrot, the waltz and the big band sound, with the unforgettable strains of 'We'll Meet Again' drifting from the Cricketers' Tavern.

Following her Channel crossing the *Canberra* docked at Cherbourg early on the morning of Monday 6 June and her passengers were able to disembark to revisit the beaches of 1944 and remember both the momentous events of 50 years previously and their fallen comrades who did not return home. Despite some talk of a strike by French dock workers, there were no problems and both the *Canberra* and *QE2* were given a warm welcome amidst the dismal drizzle, and the local police band played some stirring French military music on the quayside. The cruise ended at Southampton on the morning of Tuesday 7 June 1994, and that same evening the *Canberra* returned to her scheduled cruising programme with a 10-night voyage to the Atlantic Islands.

As the end of the year approached plans were put in hand for the *Canberra's* annual refit, which included a major investment in her engine room machinery, new bathrooms being fitted in many of the forward cabins, and the complete refurbishment of the Island Room buffet and the Cricketers' Tavern. The start of the 1995 programme was to see the entry into service of the new cruise ship, *Oriana*, and the company intended to have a three-ship operation with the new vessel running alongside the *Canberra* and the *Sea Princess*.

The *Canberra's* last cruise before her refit at Southampton was a 22-night voyage to the Caribbean, and with 1,495 passengers embarked she sailed from Southampton during the evening of Tuesday 15 November 1994. Her final port of call on the cruise was Madeira and she left Funchal, after a six-hour stay, during the afternoon of Sunday 4 December for her three-day passage back to her home port. At 1.12am on Wednesday 7 December, with St Catherine's Point Light on the most southerly point of the Isle of Wight bearing 304° and ten miles distant, the officer of the watch on the bridge began a turn to port in order to make the planned rendezvous at the pilot station at 2.30am, without the need for any further reductions in speed. At the time the wind was south-by-west and force 8 with a heavy sea, which created uncomfortable conditions for many of the passengers.

At 12.45am the ship's engineers had changed over fuel tanks for the main boilers, but this had led to severe pressure fluctuations and as a result the fuel suction pumps were changed back to the original tanks. However, at 1.25am it was noticed that the fuel oil and steam pressures were falling and standby pumps failed to pick up suction. In order to try to conserve steam pressure the main engines

The *Canberra's* final visit to San Francisco as she passes under the Golden Gate Bridge on 14 March 1997. *(Marvin Jensen)*

were slowed down and electrical load was shed in order to reduce the demand to a minimum. As the vessel lost her main propulsion an attempt was made to gain more sea-room by turning to port, but by 1.43am she had lost headway and settled heading to the west with St Catherine's Light bearing 296°, and eight and a half miles away. *Canberra's* master, Captain Rory Smith, immediately sent out a warning to other vessels in the area that his ship was not under command, and a plot of the liner's drift was started.

Because of the lack of steam pressure the turbo-alternators tripped off the switchboard, which in turn blacked out the ship and caused some consternation to passengers. However, the emergency diesel generator started automatically and this supplied power to the essential services. At 1.45am Captain Smith informed passengers of the situation over the public address system, and in addition the Deputy Captain and other officers visited all the public rooms to reassure passengers. Fortunately, with most passengers asleep or preferring to remain in their cabins, the public rooms were generally quiet, but those who did remain in the public spaces were

kept informed of the developing situation. During her passage up the Channel, ballast had been moved to counteract the effect of the strong wind on the starboard side of the vessel. When she settled on her westerly heading, the offset ballast, combined with the wind which was now blowing on the port side, caused the vessel to list 4° to starboard, which increased the discomfort of the passengers, and in some cases, their state of alarm as well, but fortunately, did not add to the danger.

At 1.52am a request was sent out for tugs to assist and 15 minutes later the Coastguard confirmed that a tug was on its way. By 2.20am the tide was having a greater effect on the drift of the vessel and the coastline was now only four and a half miles away. Twenty minutes later, at 2.40am, with the vessel continuing to drift north-westerly towards the bank at the south of St Catherine's Deep, final preparations for anchoring were made and the port anchor was let go at 2.51am. However, it soon became clear that the *Canberra* was dragging this anchor and at 3.01am the starboard anchor was dropped and run out to eight shackles of cable. Fortunately, this virtually stopped the drift and by this time steam pressure on the main boilers was being regained.

At 3.55am full power was once more available to the main propulsion motors and orders were given to weigh anchor. Unfortunately, it was found that the port anchor was fouled with the starboard cable and it took almost two hours to clear the tangle. By this time however, the tug *Bustler* was standing by and three others were being held in the eastern approaches to the Solent. Fortunately, they were not required and at 6.22am the ship was once again under way and she was able to continue her passage to the Nab Tower where the pilot boarded at 7.24am. Just over three hours later, at 10.30am, the *Canberra* berthed safely alongside the quay in Southampton's Western Docks.

By this time the press had realized that the incident might provide a good story and reporters were keen to interview the disembarking passengers. It quickly became public knowledge that six of the refitting contractor's staff had joined the ship at Barbados and rumours began to circulate that one of the *Canberra's* main engines had been stripped down and was not operational. However, a subsequent inquiry by the Marine Accident Investigation Branch (MAIB) of the Department of Transport soon scotched these rumours and confirmed that all the *Canberra's* main propulsion machinery was in use or readily available if required.

However, the investigation by the MAIB did conclude that a degree of confusion existed in the engine room during the early stages of the emergency, with an apparent lack of an effective command structure. It also found an initial reluctance to communicate with the Coastguard until contact had been made with the P&O management, which was exacerbated by problems in settling up a communications link with the shore staff. It also went on to note that it would have been much more prudent to have anchored the vessel during the early stages of the incident, but that the master's reasons for not doing so were understandable and were based on his many years of experience on the vessel, and consideration of all the factors known to him. The Inquiry concluded its findings by stating: 'In general the safety and care of passengers was kept in the forefront of the master's mind even though he was beset with both navigational and communications problems.'

Fortunately, the *Canberra's* Christmas and New Year cruise and her 1995 world voyage passed off without incident, apart from three stowaways who were found early in the latter cruise, and the liner returned to Southampton on the morning of Friday 7 April 1995 to join the brand new *Oriana* which had arrived in the port four days earlier after a controversial two weeks following her departure from the builder's yard. She had been due to arrive at noon on Sunday 26 March, but on her first and most critical voyage, a passage down the River Ems through northern Germany to the open sea, her keel scraped the river bottom. This was in spite of the fact that the river had been

specially dredged, the ship herself had pumped out oil and water, and her lifeboats had been removed to shed weight and, in addition, heavy rain had raised the river level by three inches. Electricity supplies to a large area of Lower Saxony had to be rerouted in order to allow power cables which crossed the river to be tied together and lifted out of the way, giving the ship's yellow funnel an extra nine inches of clearance. During the passage she passed between the arches of a railway bridge that had been dismantled and even then there were only a few feet to spare. The departure of the new ship was marked by a day of celebration, with people travelling for many miles to watch her progress downriver. However, with stormy weather conditions in the North Sea and with excessive vibration from her giant propellers which, it appeared, had been damaged during her passage down the River Ems, delays had been caused which resulted in her late arrival at Southampton. Fortunately, the naming ceremony - the modern version of the traditional launching ceremony - was performed on Thursday 6 April and two days later the *Canberra* left for the Caribbean and the start of her UK cruising season. Seventeen cruises later, which included a visit to the North Cape and a three-day break to Le Havre and Cherbourg, she made her final cruise of the season - a 22-night Christmas and New Year cruise, once again to the Caribbean. The 1995 season had seen P&O operating three large cruise ships from the port of Southampton for the first time since 1976, when the *Arcadia* had briefly joined the *Canberra* and the old *Oriana*, which was an indication that cruising was well established and, indeed, was the strongest growing sector of the holiday industry.

However, by the start of her 1996 cruise season, rumours of *Canberra's* imminent demise were circulating and on Tuesday 25 June 1996, as the cruise ship steamed home to Southampton from Vigo on her sixth cruise of the season, P&O made the announcement which was to mark the end of an era - that the *Canberra* would conclude her long and distinguished career with P&O on Tuesday 30 September 1997. Perhaps the most surprising aspect of the announcement was that the ship which was destined to replace the *Canberra* was the 63,524-gross ton diesel-electric ship *Star Princess*. She had been ordered for Sitmar Cruises and constructed for the Italian company by Chartiers de l'Atlantique, at St Nazaire, France. She was launched on 5 March 1988 as the *Sitmar Fairmajesty*, but four months later P&O acquired the Sitmar company when its shareholders agreed to sell all their stock in a deal which was negotiated with the chairman of the trust which managed the Italian cruise company. The vessel was completed in March 1989 and she arrived at Port Everglades on the 17th of that month. Six days later, at a dockside ceremony in the port, the Hollywood film star Audrey Hepburn christened the ship *Star Princess*. She sailed on her maiden voyage, a ten-day Caribbean cruise,

Canberra's place in the UK cruise market is to be taken by the Italian-built *Star Princess*, which has been renamed *Arcadia*. She certainly has a hard act to follow. *(A. Hernandez)*

on 24 May and she continued her career with Princess Cruises with a series of short cruises from Port Everglades. P&O finally renamed the ship *Arcadia* in readiness for her transfer to the UK cruising scene.

The *Canberra's* final season opened on Monday 6 January 1997, when she left Southampton for her last world voyage which took her on what used to be P&O's traditional route to the Far East by way of the Mediterranean Sea and the Suez Canal. After leaving the Red Sea she steamed east across the Arabian Sea to Bombay, before sailing on to Port Kelang and Keppel Harbour in Singapore. On Sunday 23 February she made her final call at Sydney where, accompanied by tugs, firefloats and small boats of every kind, she received a warm welcome in the harbour. She returned to Southampton by way of the West Coast of the USA and Panama, arriving in her home port early on the morning of Monday 7 April to begin her final series of 12 cruises to familiar destinations.

The *Canberra* made her final passenger departure from Southampton during the evening of Wednesday 10 September 1997, for a 20-day cruise to Mediterranean

ports which had become so familiar during her years as a cruise ship. Her sailing did not go unnoticed, with the event being covered by the news media and witnessed by many of her loyal followers.

When the *Canberra* arrived back in British waters on the morning of Tuesday 30 September, the whole area was blanketed in an all-enveloping fog with the visibility reduced to less than 200 yards. However, the welcome which was to be afforded to this most British of cruise ships was not going to be spoiled by the autumn mist, and from the early hours of the morning thousands of people packed the waterfront vantage points, from Southampton's Mayflower Park to Calshot Castle, where Southampton Water meets the Solent. The first salute came from Royal Navy warships which were off the south coast carrying out the annual Staff College Sea Days exercise. Despite the fact that they could hardly be seen, the destroyers *Birmingham*, *Edinburgh* and *Southampton*, together with the frigates *Cornwall* and *Lancaster*, all with their decks fully manned, made their ceremonial sail-past. Spectators on the Isle of Wight were disappointed since the *Canberra* was hardly visible as she steamed through the Solent, but at 10.15am,

The *Canberra's* final resting place, at Gaddani Beach, Pakistan, on the shores of the Arabian Sea. She has been deliberately run aground and small boats are being used to remove all remaining stores and equipment. As she becomes lighter and rises in the water she will be pulled closer inshore.
(Popperfoto/Reuters)

as she passed Calshot Castle and turned into Southampton Water, the mist began to lift and the bright sunshine of what was to be a warm autumn day shone through to reveal the great white liner dressed overall and proudly flying a 37 metre-long paying-off pennant from her mast - one metre for every year of her life. The frigate HMS *Cornwall* followed in her wake with hundreds of small boats clustered round, all eager to add their salute. Her passengers, despite the inevitable sadness of the occasion, had entered into the spirit of the day and had made scores of banners during the voyage which now decorated the ship's rails, creating a scene reminiscent of her homecoming from the Falkland Islands 15 years earlier.

At 11am exactly the sightseers on Hythe Pier got their first glimpse of the unique shape of the *Canberra,* preceded by two firefloats and followed by HMS *Cornwall*, as she loomed out of the mist. All the accompanying craft, which included the two larger, but elderly steamers *Waverley* and *Shieldhall*, both of which were packed with eager spectators, sounded their whistles and sirens in salute. A few minutes later, as she passed Mayflower Park, the Parachute Regiment's freefall team paid their own spectacular tribute to the great ship as they parachuted from only 8,500 feet with pinpoint accuracy into the park. One member of the team recalled how, as a 22-year-old corporal, he had sailed to the South Atlantic in the liner, and how he had last seen her being strafed by enemy aircraft as she lay in San Carlos Water: 'She looked almost unreal, as though she had been superimposed there because she looked so big compared to the other ships. Today, when I jumped out of the plane, I wasn't looking at the dropping zone but at *Canberra's* swimming pool.'

As the *Canberra* turned off the port's Western Docks before being manoeuvred into her berth, a lone RAF Canberra bomber roared overhead in a dramatic low-level fly-past, making a salute from a veteran of the air to a veteran of the sea. It was followed in quick succession by two Royal Navy Sea King helicopters and a V formation of army Lynx helicopters. As she approached the dockhead the party on board was in full swing with passengers and crew members dancing and waving as thousands of balloons, clouds of coloured smoke and fireworks swirled into the sky from the liner's decks. Then, with her siren sounding every few minutes, the *Canberra* started the complicated series of manoeuvres which would bring her into 106 berth for the last time. By 12.15pm the great ship was secured alongside and Captain Rory Smith had rung 'Finished With Engines'. The party was over and the disembarkation of passengers began.

Next day, for the first time in her 37-year career, the *Canberra* had become something of a liability in the port and even the local Southampton newspaper omitted her from their list of 'Ships in Port'. That evening she had to vacate 106 berth in order to make room for P&O's new cruise ship, *Oriana*, which was returning from a 12-day Mediterranean cruise and so, at 7pm on a dark autumn evening, after the *QE2* had departed her berth for a transatlantic voyage to New York, the *Canberra* was shifted, almost surreptitiously, across to the Eastern Docks where destoring could begin. During her final nine days alongside at Southampton, as well as stores, many works of art and mementoes were removed from the ship and packed carefully into containers to be dispatched to the *Canberra's* birthplace, the Harland & Wolff shipyard at Belfast, where they could be transferred to the old lady's successor, *Arcadia*, where many of them would feature in a 'Canberra Room' on board.

On the morning of Friday 10 October 1997, in a brief two-line Press Release, the *Canberra's* death knell was sounded when it was announced that the once great ship had been sold to a scrap merchant at Karachi, Pakistan, and that she would leave Southampton that same evening. The final, one-way, voyage began at 9pm that evening when her mooring ropes were slipped and tugs pulled her slowly away from the quayside. Her skeleton crew was commanded by Captain Mike Carr and as she edged slowly down Southampton Water he gave three farewell blasts on the siren. From her brilliantly lit, but strangely deserted and silent decks, came the melancholy sound of a piper's lament whilst on shore a small crowd had gathered to see her off. This time there were no passengers, no farewell bands or streamers, just the memories of almost four decades of service. It was all in such sharp contrast to the welcome she had received just ten days before and by midnight the pilot had been disembarked and the *Canberra* had left British shores for ever as she set sail on her last 20-day voyage from which there would be no return.

The *Canberra* was bound for Gaddani, about 30 miles north-west of Karachi, and the largest shipbreaking centre in the world. However, it is not a port in the accepted sense, but all the old ships are grounded a hundred yards or so from the sandy beaches where they are virtually dismantled by hand. *Canberra* arrived off Gaddani at the end of October and once she was firmly aground the process of unloading the remaining stores and the ship's equipment began, using small boats to provide a shuttle service between the beach and the accommodation ladder at the after end of D Deck on the starboard side.

It was a sad end for such a great ship, but the *Canberra* will always be remembered as one of the greatest of ocean liners and her legend will remain forever in the annals of British maritime history.

The *Canberra's* 'finest hour' as on Sunday 11 July 1982, in the full gaze of the whole world's media, she returns in triumph to a tremendous reception at Southampton from the campaign in the South Atlantic. *(P&O)*

Principal Particulars (As Built)

Length Overall:	820ft
Length B P:	740ft
Breadth:	102ft
Gross Tonnage:	45,000
Cargo Capacity:	150,000 cu ft
Main Prop Machinery:	Twin propellers driven by electric motors powered by two BT-H turbo-alternators. Steam provided by three Foster Wheeler external superheater D-type boilers at 750psi & 960°F. 85,000 SHP.
Service Speed:	$27\frac{1}{2}$ knots
Passengers:-	
First Class:	548
Tourist Class:	1,690
One class (cruising)	1,641
Crew:	960

Acknowledgements

Mr T. K. Anderson, Ulster Folk & Transport Museum: Mr Peter Ashton, *Southern Daily Echo*, Southampton, Hampshire: Mr E. A. Azab, Chief of Public Relations, Suez Canal Authority, Ismailia, Egypt: Mr Roger Beacham, Cheltenham Reference Library: Captain Michael V. N. Bradford RD RNR, P&O: Mr Monty Beckett, Southampton, Hampshire: Photographic Librarian, *Belfast Telegraph*, Belfast: Miss J. Bevin, Vosper Thorneycroft Ltd, Southampton: Ian Blackwell/Sylvia Duffin, Popperfoto, Northampton: Mr Norman Brouwer, Historian, South Street Seaport Museum, New York, USA: Mr Michael Cassar, Valletta, Malta: Mr David Cole, Ventnor, Isle of Wight: Mr Ernie Cole, North Harrow, Middlesex: Mr Brian Conroy, Greatham, Hampshire: Kay Davidson, P&O, London: Mr Derek Deere, *Shipping World & Shipbuilder*, Marine Publications International Ltd, Basingstoke, Hampshire: Mr Francis J. Duffy, Valley Stream, New York, USA: Carol Farr, *The News*, Portsmouth, Hampshire: Ambrose Greenway, London: Mr R. B. Grice, Salisbury, Wiltshire: Mr Alan Hale, P&O: Mr Andres Hernandez, Miami, Florida, USA: Mr Mark Histed, MoD Northwood, Middlesex: Mr Marvin Jensen, Santa Cruz, California, USA: Mr Peter Knego, Moor Park, California, USA: Mr Matthew Little, Royal Marines Museum, Eastney, Hampshire: Mr Bert Moody, Southampton, Hampshire: Mr George Mortimore, Ryde, Isle of Wight: Mr Peter J. G. Mumford, Beken Maritime Services, Cowes, Isle of Wight: Commander John. L. Muxworthy RN, MoD Northwood, Middlesex: Commander J. J. Nicholas RN (Retd), Exton, Hampshire: Mrs Lyn Palmer, P&O, London: Mr Anthony Perrett, Royal Marines Historical Society, Eastney, Hampshire: Mr Norman Pound, P&O Chief Engineer, Poulton Le Fylde: Mr Stephen Rabson, P&O, London: Mr Robert Shopland, *Ships Monthly*, Burton-on-Trent, Staffordshire: Mr Ian Spashett, Folkestone, Kent: Mr Daryl Stevens, Cooloongup, Western Australia: Mr R. G. Todd, National Maritime Museum, London. Finally to my wife Freda, my niece Tara Murphy, University of Sydney, Australia, and to my daughters Caroline and Louise for all their help.

Special Thanks Must Go To:
Mr Brian Conroy, Greatham, Hampshire, for his fine watercolour painting on the front cover.
Mr Derek Deere, Managing Director, Marine Publications International Ltd, Basingstoke, Hampshire, for permission to use the General Arrangement Deck Plans which were originally published in the June 1961 souvenir issue of *Shipbuilder & Marine Engine Builder*.
Mr John S. Morris, Dalgety Bay, Fife, for the fine pen & ink drawing on the front endpaper.
George Mortimore, Action Photos, 17 Marlborough Close, Ryde, Isle of Wight, for permission to use his excellent 'action' shots of *Canberra* on her way to the South Atlantic, copies of which can be obtained from him at the above address.
Mr Ian Spashett, Director, FotoFlite, for permission to use his company's photographs, copies of which can be obtained direct from FotoFlite, New Romney, Kent, TN28 8LW.

Bibliography

A Hundred Year History of the P&O: Boyd Cable: Ivor Nicholson & Watson Ltd: 1937.
These Splendid Ships - The Story of the Peninsular & Oriental Line: David Divine: Frederick Muller Ltd: 1960.
Beneath The Houseflag of the P&O: Peter Padfield: Hutchinson: 1981.
Canberra - The Great White Whale Goes To War: Lt Cdr J. L. Muxworthy RN: P&O SN Co: 1982.
P&O In the Falklands - The Pictorial Record: Stephen Rabson: P&O SN Co: 1982.
SS *Canberra* - The Great White Whale: Shipbuilder Magazine & Neil McCart: Patrick Stephens Ltd: 1983.
From *Chusan* to *Sea Princess*: Malcolm R. Gordon: Allen & Unwin: 1985.
20th Century Passenger Ships of the P&O: Neil McCart: Patrick Stephens Ltd: 1985.
Passenger Ships of the Orient Line: Neil McCart: Patrick Stephens Ltd: 1987.
The Story of P&O: David & Stephen Howarth: Weidenfeld & Nicholson: 1986.
About Ourselves & Wavelength - Staff Magazines of the P&O.
Newspapers: The Times, London: Lloyds List & Shipping Gazette, London: Daily Telegraph, London: The Times of Malta: New York Times: Shipbuilder & Marine Engine Builder: Sydney Morning Herald, Australia: The Straits Times, Singapore: Daily Mail, London: Daily Mirror, London: The News, Portsmouth: The Southern Daily Echo, Southampton: San Francisco Chronicle.
P&O Records held at the National Maritime Museum: Department of Trade, Department of Transport and Admiralty Records held at the Public Record Office, Kew, London: Records held by the Marine Accident Investigation Branch of the Department of Transport, London.

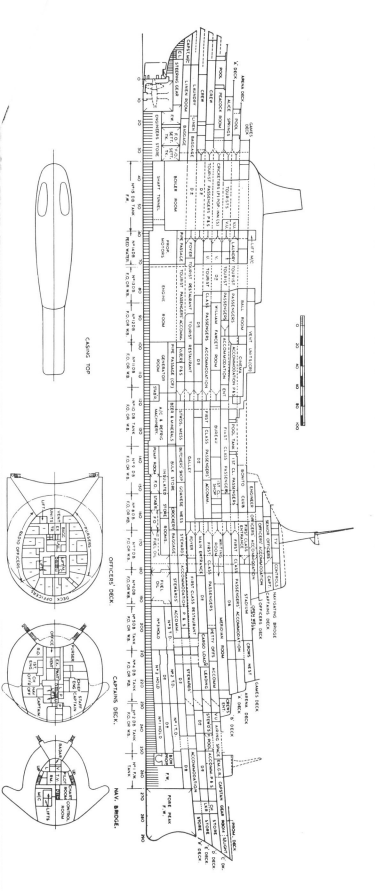

GENERAL ARRANGEMENT OF THE "CANBERRA"